CW00500767

CHARMING
SMALL HOTEL
GUIDES

Austria

CHARMING SMALL HOTEL GUIDES

Austria

Edited by Kathy Arnold & Paul Wade

DUNCAN PETERSEN

HUNTER
PUBLISHING INC

Originally published in 1993, reprinted 1995, revised and updated 1997, 1999

5th printing published 2000 by
Duncan Petersen Publishing Ltd,
31 Ceylon Road, London W14 OPY

Conceived, designed and produced by Duncan Petersen
Edited by Team Wade

Editors Paul Wade, Kathy Arnold
Art Director Mel Petersen

Sales representation and distribution in the UK and Ireland by
Portfolio Books Ltd
Unit 1c West Ealing Business Centre
Alexandria Road
London W13 ONJ
Tel: 0181 579 7748

ISBN 1-872576-86-9

A CIP catalogue record for this book is available from the British Library

AND

Published in the USA by
Hunter Publishing Inc.,
130 Campus Drive, Edison, N.J. 08818.
Tel (732) 225 1900 Fax (732) 417 0482
For details on hundreds of other travel guides and language courses, visit Hunter's Web site at www.hunterpublishing.com

ISBN 1-55650-898-0

Originated by Reprocolor International S.R.I., Milan
Printed by Stige, Turin

Contents

Introduction

This is a new edition in the well-established series of Charming Small Hotel Guides. Austria's natural beauty, combined with its history and culture, makes it one of the most alluring tourist destinations.To complete that idyllic experience, a charming, small, family-run hotel is essential. We have over 250 listed here, most with fewer than 30 rooms ranging from total luxury to rustic simplicity, from city to mountain-side, from lakeside to vineyard. All have a warmth of welcome, a desire to make guests comfortable and the willingness to go an extra step to please.

Entries

In this volume, our warmest recommendations are reflected in the full-page reports. Following these are shorter entries, four to a page. These are not 'second class' hotels, but for one reason or another do not justify a full page.

Bedrooms

Many of our readers prefer the comfort of their own separate bed and are keen to know about twin-bedded bedrooms. In most hotels, the traditional Austrian double bed is essentially two singles, pushed together, with separate mattresses and separate duvets. We found that a true 'double bed' was a rarity.

Public rooms

From the smallest tavern to the grandest castle hotel, the *Stube* is an essential ingredient. Usually wood-panelled, this room, with its bench seats, large tables and *Kachelofen* (ceramic stove) is the place to eat, drink and relax.

Meals

Breakfast is usually a buffet, an enterprising mixture of fresh and dried fruits, cereals, cold meats and cheeses with a variety of fresh rolls and breads. Eating in at night is an excellent way to meet both the host and other guests who stay on to chat in the *Stube* after dinner over a fiery glass of *Schnaps.*

Bio

Austria is an environmentally-aware nation. In hotels and restaurants, *Bio* indicates the use of wholefood or organic products. *Bio* rooms are furnished in natural materials, and some have master-switches that cut off all electric current during the night to ensure a natural night's sleep.

Smoking

Smoking is still a popular vice, with only a handful of hotels able to offer non-smoking dining areas or bedrooms.

Introduction

Electricity
Few of the hotels listed have 'international' sockets, so adaptors are essential for visitors with electric razors.

Credit cards
Austrian hoteliers are fighting a battle with the major credit card companies, over their charge rates. They prefer to take Eurocheques, travellers cheques, even cash.

Your host and hostess
Most inn-keepers enjoy being involved with their guests, whether it is cross-country skiing or hiking, tasting wines or teaching cookery. Pleasant as an overnight stay will be, a longer visit will always give added insight into the local family or region.

Travel facts
The staff at the Austrian National Tourist Offices around the world are particularly helpful to the individual traveller when it comes to special interest holidays. Contact the Austrian National Tourist Office in Britain at: PO Box 2363, London, W1A 2QB. Tel: (0171) 629 0461; fax: (0171) 499 6038. E-mail: oewlon@easynet.co.uk In the United States write to: PO Box 1142, New York, N.Y. 10108. Tel: (212) 944 6880; fax: (212) 730 4568. On the Internet: http://austria-info.at/

Flights and Car Hire
Lauda Air, owned by former world champion motor-racing driver Niki Lauda, is based in Vienna, and is served by fifteen flights a week from the UK. Four flights a week depart Gatwick's South Terminal, with eleven flights a week from Manchester International Airport. Lauda Air provides the only scheduled service from the UK to Salzburg operating twelve times a week from London Gatwick aboard 50-seat executive-style Canadair Regional Jets featuring award-winning service and cuisine.

Lauda Air also flies to Miami and 13 European cities. Their Fly & Drive Package allows customers in both Amadeus and economy class the convenience of being able to reserve a Hertz car when they book their flight, or on arrival at their destination.

How to find an entry
Entries are arranged geographically. Austria is divided into 5 regions; we start in Western Austria and move clockwise through North-western, North-eastern, Eastern and finally Southern Austria. Each of our regions consists of one or more of the nine provinces that make up Austria.

Introduction

Each section dedicated to a region follows a set sequence:
First comes an introduction to the province.

Then come the main, full-page entries for that province, listed in alphabetical order by town.

Finally come the shorter, quarter-page entries for that province, again listed in alphabetical order by town.

There are three easy ways to find a hotel:
Use the maps between pages 10 and 19. The numbers refer to the page in the book where a hotel is listed.

If you know which province you are visiting, browse through that section until you find a place that fits the bill.

Use the indexes which list entries both by place name (p187-191) and by hotel name (p184-186).

How to read an entry
At the top of the page is the area of Austria; below that is the name of the provincee; then follows the type of hotel, its town and finally, the hotel itself.

The snowflake ❄
We have added the snowflake to help you recognize hotels catering for winter sports. All have ski-rooms.

Fact boxes
Beneath each hotel description are the facts and figures which should help you to decide whether or not the hotel is in your price range and has the facilities that you require. Do confirm prices when you make your reservation.

Tel When dialling from abroad, use 43 (the international code) followed by the number, omitting the initial 0. Within Austria, dial the number shown.

Fax Most hotels now have a fax number which makes reservations swifter and easier.

Location The setting of the hotel is described briefly; car parking facilities follow.

Meals Most hotels offer all meals, but we have included some bed-and-breakfasts, too.

Prices These show two prices - from the cheapest single room in low season to the most expensive double room in high season. Do ask proprietors about special reductions. We have coded the prices in bands:

S	- under 500 Austrian Schillings
SS	- 500 to 1000 Austrian Schillings
SSS	- 1000 to 1500 Austrian Schillings
SSSS	- over 1500 Austrian Schillings

In the Kleinwalsertal where German marks are the currency:

M	- under 50 Deutschmarks
MM	- 50 to 100 Deutschmarks
MMM	- 100 to 200 Deutschmarks
MMMM	- over 200 Deutschmarks

Rooms We summarize the number and style of bedrooms available. Our lists of facilities in bedrooms do not cover ornaments such as flowers or consumables such as toiletries.

Facilities We list public rooms as well as outdoor and sporting facilities which are either part of the hotel or close by; facilities in the vicinity of the hotel feature at the end of the main section under **Nearby**.

Credit cards We use the following abbreviations for credit cards:

AE	American Express,
DC	Diners Club,
MC	Master Card (Access/Eurocard),
V	Visa (Barclaycard/Bank Americard/Carte Bleue)

Proprietors Where managers are employed, we name them.

Glossary of terms

Several German terms are used in our hotel descriptions.

Alm	mountain hut
Apartment	large bedroom with extra sitting area
Bio	organic natural food; sometimes bedrooms where only natural fibres and materials are used
Kachelofen	traditional ceramic-tiled stove
Kur	'cure'; like a health-farm
Schloss	castle
See	lake
Stammtisch	table for regulars, locals
Strudel	Austria's famous dessert, served at all times; sometimes savoury
Stube, Stüble, Stüberl	wood-panelled room where food and drinks are served
Tafelspitz	boiled beef; along with Schnitzel, a national dish

Hotel location maps

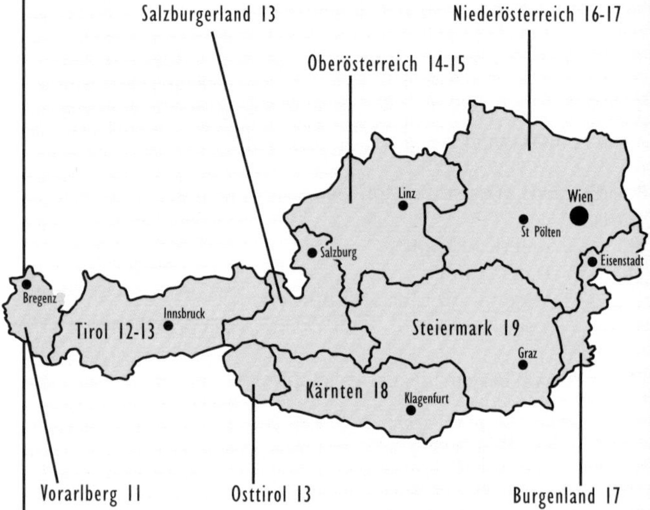

Hotel location maps

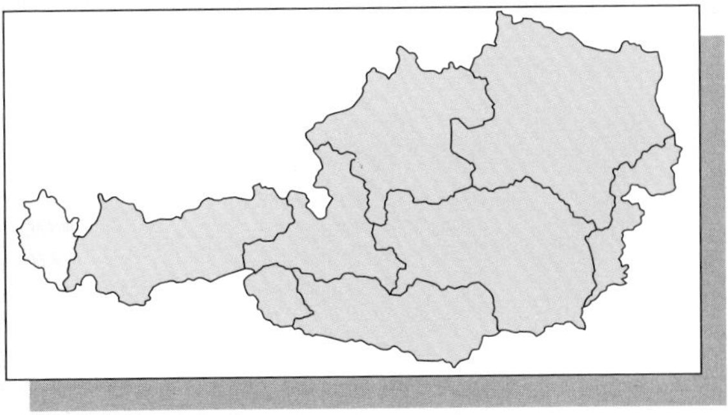

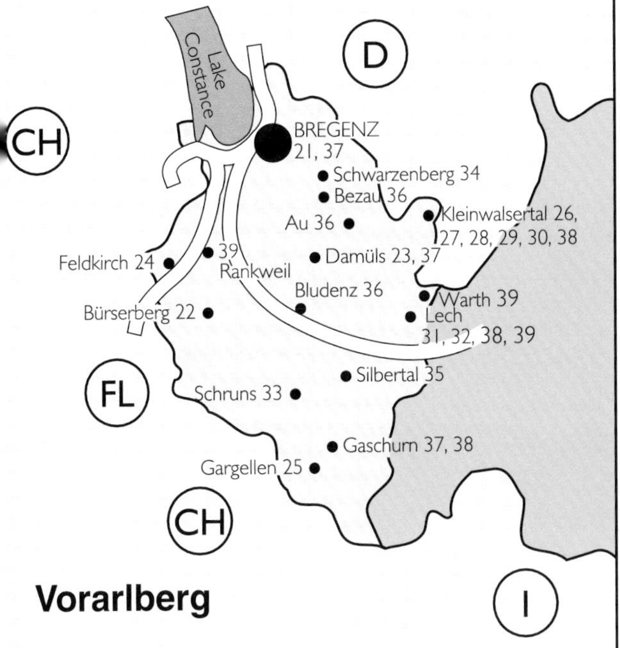

Vorarlberg

Hotel location maps

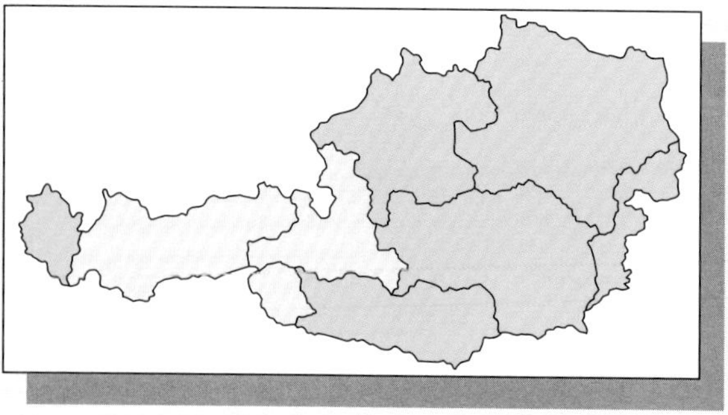

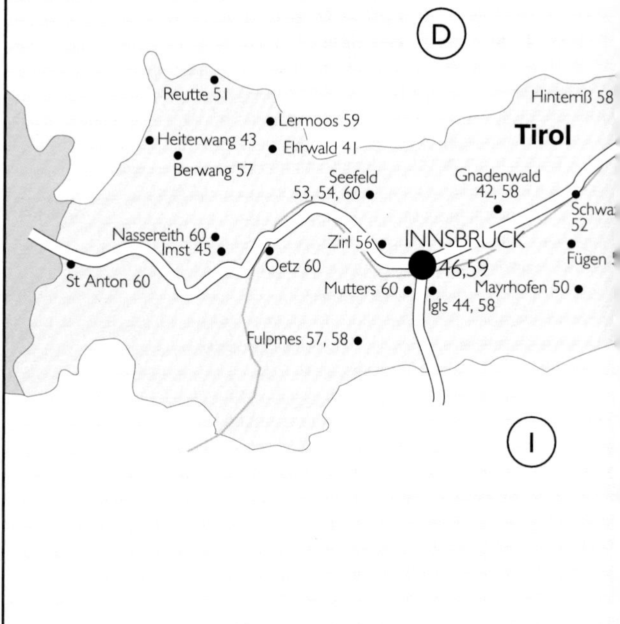

Mattsee 68
Straßwalchen 84
Salzburgerland
D
SALZBURG
70-76, 84
Fuschl am See 82
St Gilgen 77
Ebbs 57
Oberalm 84
Hallein 83
Kufstein
48, 59
Werfen 79
Filzmoos 65
Kitzbühel 59
Leogang 67, 83
Goldegg 66, 83
Altenmarkt 82
Zell 80, 81, 85
Wagrain 85
Wald
78, 85
Mittersill
69, 84
Kaprun 83
Dorfgastein 82
Badgastein
63, 64, 82
Kals 47
Matrei 60
OSTTIROL
Lienz 49
Strassen 55

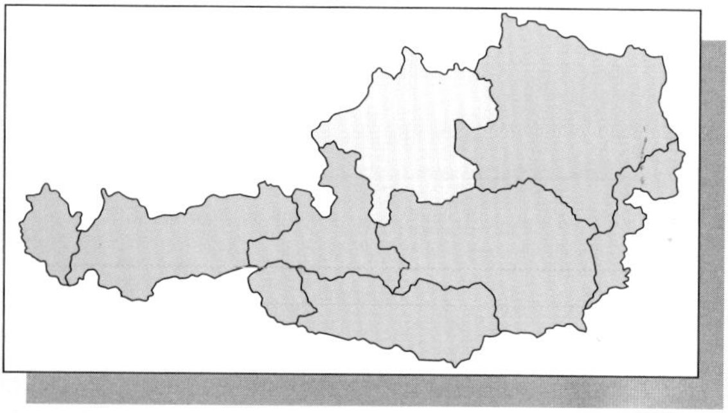

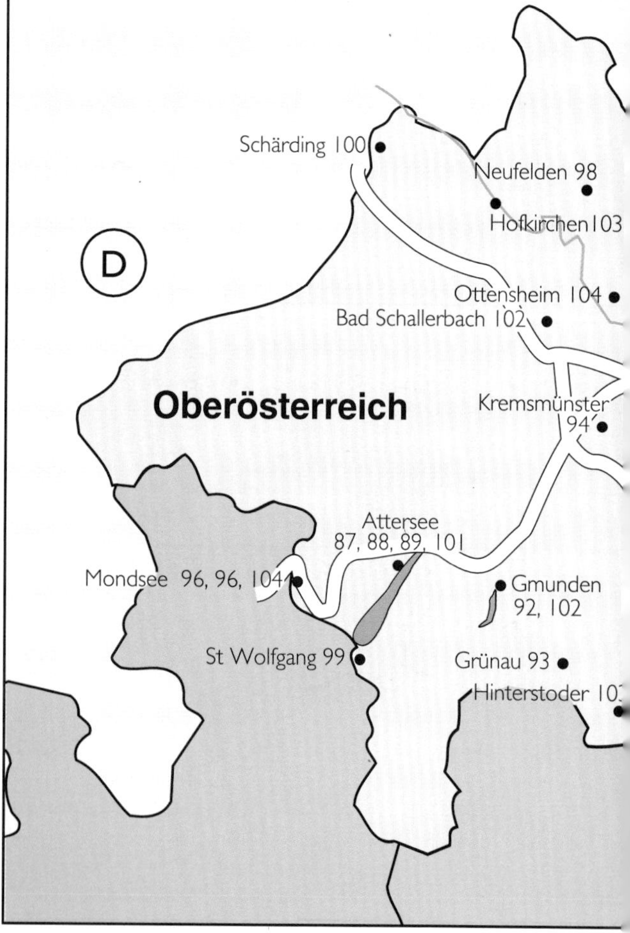
Schärding 100
Neufelden 98
Hofkirchen 103
D
Ottensheim 104
Bad Schallerbach 102
Oberösterreich
Kremsmünster 94
Attersee 87, 88, 89, 101
Mondsee 96, 96, 104
Gmunden 92, 102
St Wolfgang 99
Grünau 93
Hinterstoder

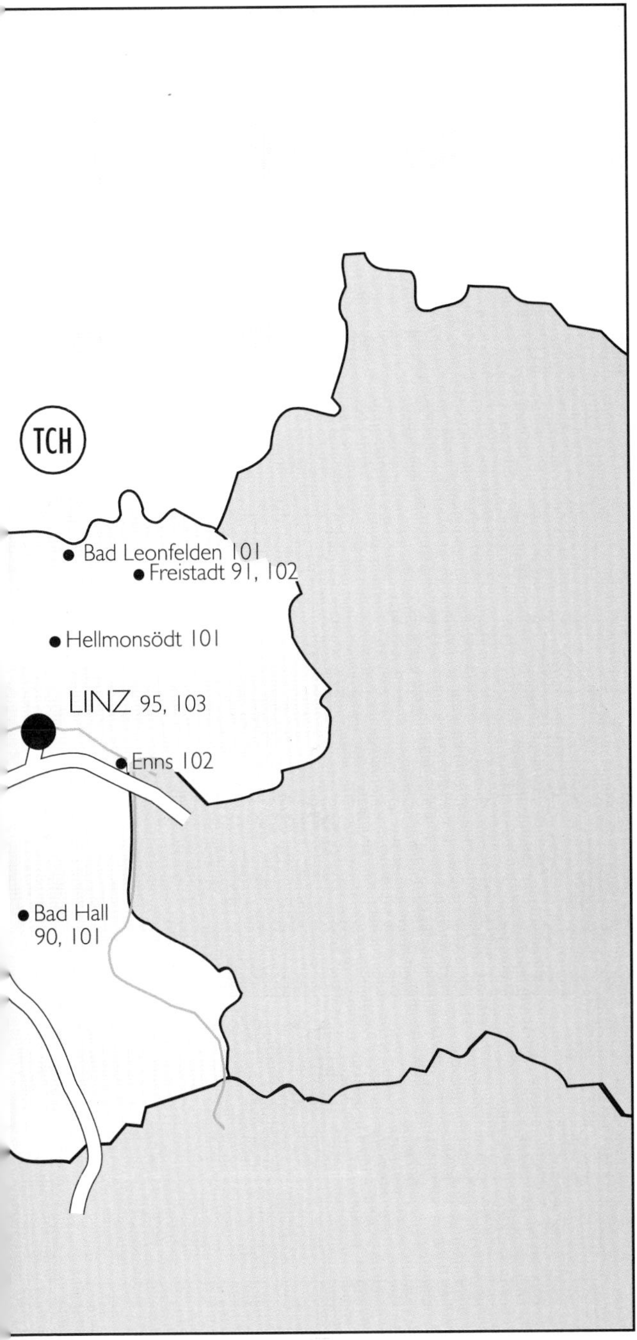
TCH
Bad Leonfelden 101
Freistadt 91, 102
Hellmonsödt 101
LINZ 95, 103
Enns 102
Bad Hall
90, 101

Hotel location maps

Hotel location maps

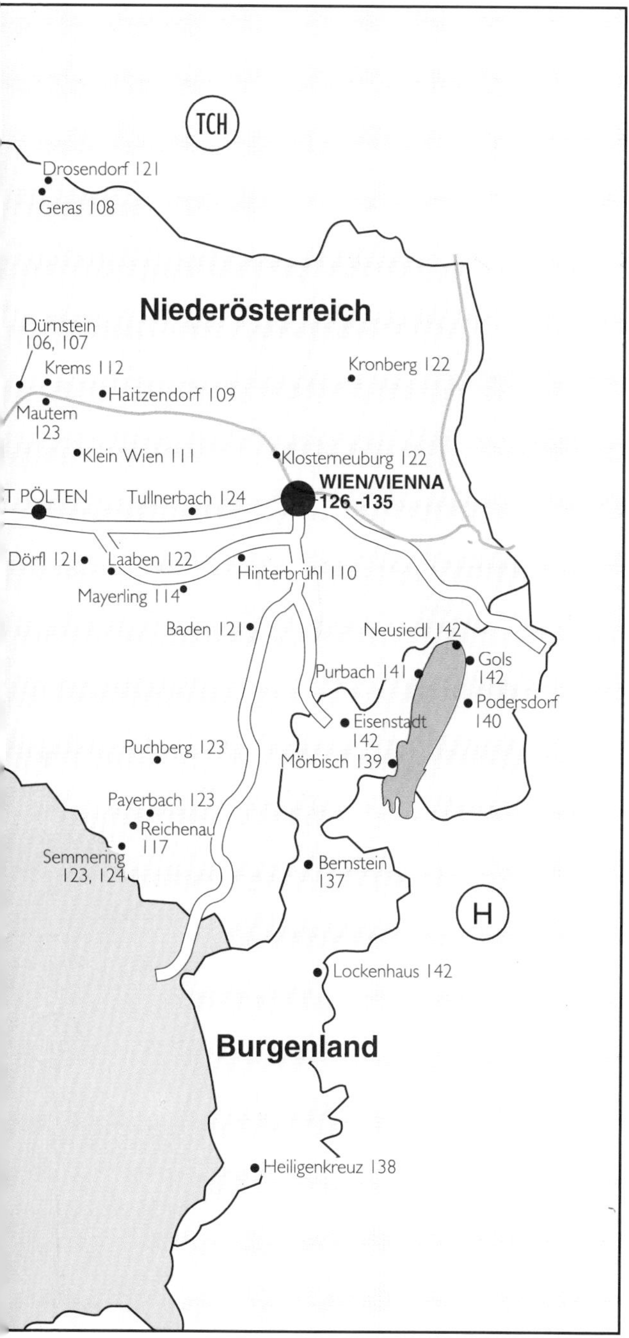

Hotel location maps

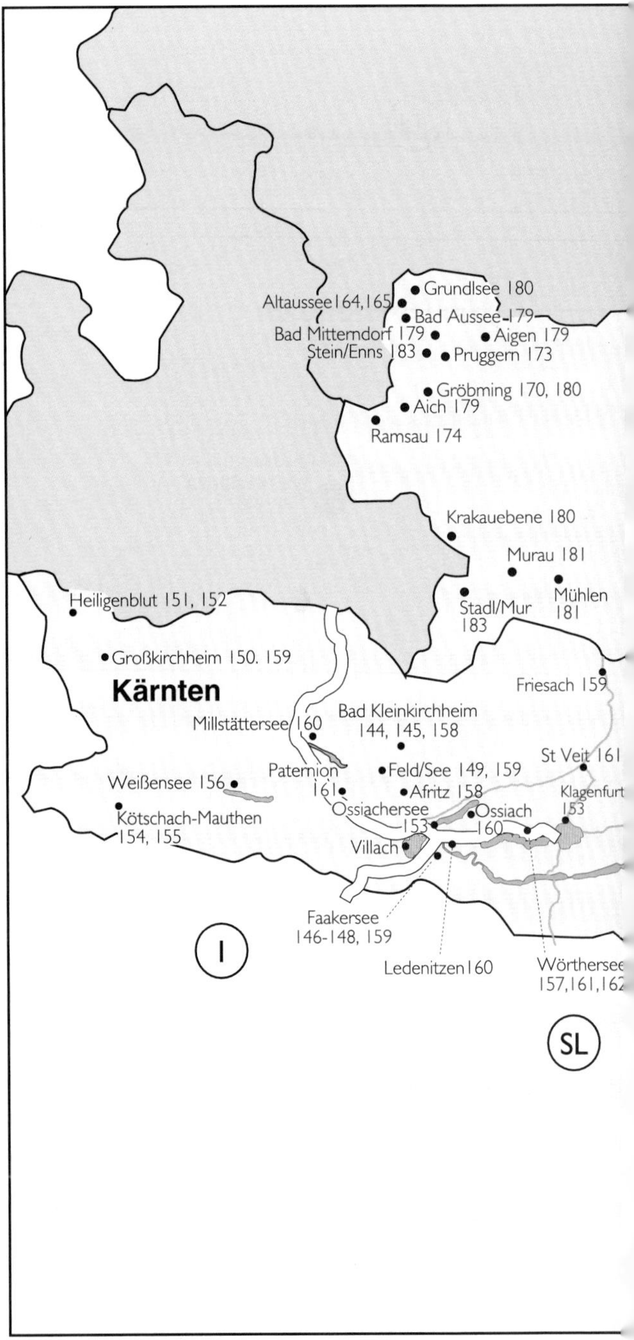

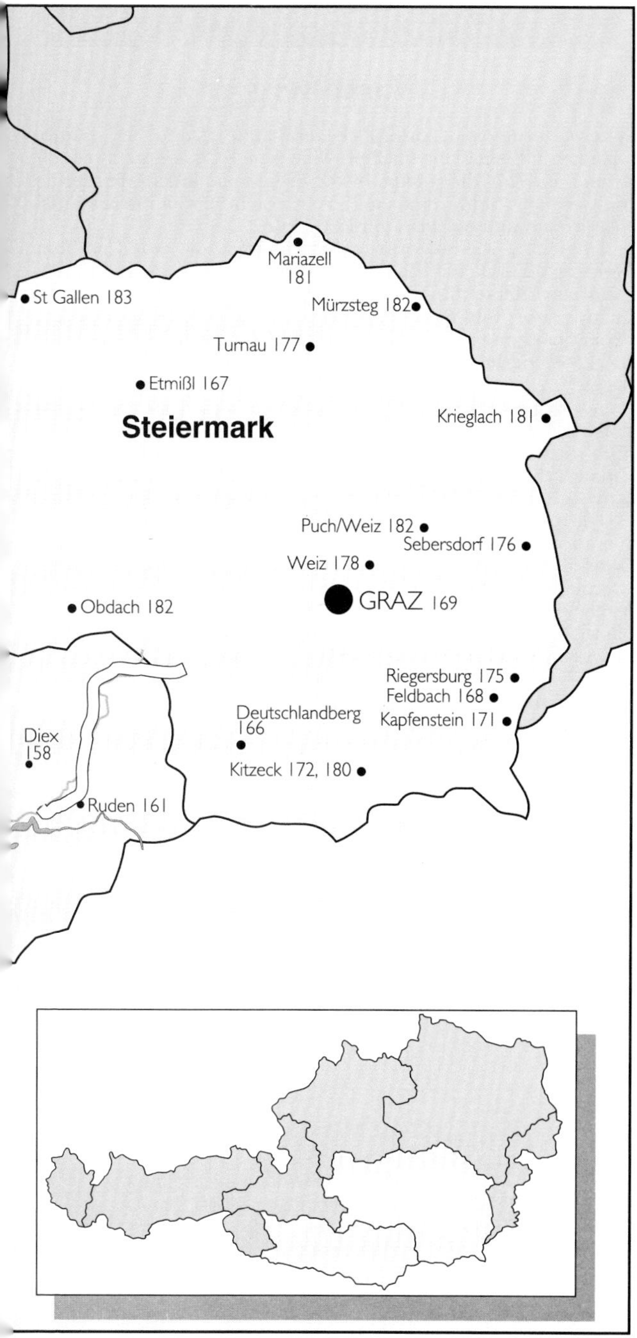
Mariazell 181
St Gallen 183
Mürzsteg 182
Turnau 177
Etmißl 167
Steiermark
Krieglach 181
Puch/Weiz 182
Sebersdorf 176
Weiz 178
GRAZ 169
Obdach 182
Riegersburg 175
Feldbach 168
Deutschlandberg 166
Kapfenstein 171
Diex 158
Kitzeck 172, 180
Ruden 161

Vorarlberg

Area introduction

Vorarlberg

The westernmost of Austria's Federal States, Vorarlberg is also, apart from Vienna, the smallest. What is more, it is virtually cut off from the rest of the country by the Arlberg mountains. Bordering on Germany, Switzerland and Liechtenstein it is an international playground with excellent tourist facilities.

Ironically, the majority of the population voted to join Switzerland back in 1919, but their neighbours decided against it. Austrians refer to this province as the *Ländle,* the little country, and many visitors find that it provides a little of everything Austrian, from opera on the lake at Bregenz to skiing in the high resort of Lech, wonderful hiking country and lazy meadows dotted with villages.

Although Vorarlberg only has access to a small strip of the vast Lake Constance, it does add a dimension to this corner of Austria. Our inspectors found hotels with dreamy views across the water. Inland, they were impressed by villages such as Schwarzenberg, with its distictive architecture and wood- shingled houses.

One unique area is the Kleinwalsertal, which is itself cut off from Vorarlberg by more high mountains. Many of the small hotels were a delight, old and reeking of atmosphere. The only road in is from Germany via Oberstdorf. Although politically part of Austria, this valley is economically part of Germany so all homes have both a German dialling code and postcode, as well as Austrian ones. Prices are quoted in Deutschmarks.

The skiing in Vorarlberg is famous throughout the world, and ranges from resorts such as Lech which attracts the rich and famous to smaller, more intimate towns such as Gargellen and Berwang.

For further details about the area, contact:
Vorarlberg-Tourismus,
State Tourist Board Vorarlberg,
Römerstrasse 7/1,
A-6901 Bregenz
Tel (05574) 425250
Fax (05574) 425255

This page acts as an introduction to the features. The long entries for this state – covering the hotels we are most enthusiastic about – start on the next page. But do not neglect the shorter entries starting on page 36: these are all hotels where we would happily stay.

Vorarlberg

Castle hotel, Bregenz

Deuring Schlössle

'Dramatic' was our reaction to this 17thC castle, up in the old part of Bregenz, overlooking Lake Constance. The scale is huge. The breakfast room looks like a medieval hall with a ceiling over 6 metres high, ancient beams, and walls over 1 metre thick. We expected to see m'lord and lady with their retinue instead of just tables and chairs beneath the swords, pikes and minstrel gallery. The bedrooms are more like suites, furnished with silk fabrics and antiques. Some are large enough for a dozen people to waltz in, others are cosier; each is special.

The food matches the surroundings. Ernst Huber was Austria's chef of the year back in 1984 when he cooked at the famous Zoll Restaurant in Bregenz. In 1989, along with his equally-talented son, Heino, he took over this castle. Like all top chefs, the Hubers use the best of local produce "but the Vorarlberg is not that rich in traditional dishes, so we invent our own or adapt ideas from chefs of the Austro-Hungarian emperors." The result is natural and light since they cut back on butter and cream. The dungeon-like wine cellar holds a valuable collection of international vintages.

Nearby old Upper Town; lake; Pfänder mountain.

6900 Bregenz, Ehre-Guta-Platz 4
Tel (05574) 47800
Fax (05574) 4780080
Location on medieval square in old town; own car parking
Meals breakfast, lunch, dinner
Prices rooms SSS-SSSS with breakfast
Rooms 13 suites; all have bath or shower, central heating, phone, TV
Facilities dining-room, sitting-room, conference room; terrace
Credit Cards AE, DC, MC, V
Children accepted
Disabled not suitable
Pets accepted; not in restaurant
Closed never
Languages English, French, Italian
Proprietors Huber family

Vorarlberg

❄ Mountain hotel, Bürserberg ❄

Berghotel Schillerkopf

'Felt at home instantly' was the reaction of our inspector, who drove up the switchbacks to reach this hotel at the end of a long day. Not only was Christine Bosek happy to show off her domaine, even other guests were welcoming. One enthused about the garden, another about the indoor swimming-pool. It is the sort of place to settle into and relax, where attention to detail ranges from hand-carved ceiling panels to bright rugs on top of wall-to-wall carpets. All this and a terrific view over Bludenz some 6 km away.

The original *Gasthof* owned by Frau Bosek's parents burned down, so the present building dates from 1977, the annexe from 1983. Sporty types are kept happy with an all-weather tennis court plus horses; in winter, guests ski out and ski back, or spend the day in one of the other resorts around Bludenz. Special events range from barbecues to a *Bauernbüffet* (country buffet), from music in the basement bar to breakfast in a forest glade.

Book one of the refurbished bedrooms, with a view over the valley or straight up the mountain. Regulars come from all age groups and from all over Europe.

Nearby winter sports, hiking, tennis, riding.

6700 Bürserberg
Tel (05552) 63104
Fax (05552) 67487
Location above Bürserberg; car parking outside
Meals breakfast, lunch, dinner, snacks
Prices rooms from S-SSS with breakfast
Rooms 8 double, 1 single, 18 suites; all have bath or shower, central heating, phone, radio; TV on request

Facilities dining-room, sitting-room, bar, TV room, table-tennis room, terrace; garden, health and fitness areas, indoor swimming-pool
Credit Cards not accepted
Children very welcome
Disabled not suitable **Pets** not accepted **Closed** Oct to mid-Dec; after Easter to mid-June
Languages English, some French
Proprietors Bosek family

Vorarlberg

❄ **Resort hotel, Damüls** ❄

Alpenhotel Mittagspitze

Two changes of ownership in the last few years might give pause for thought, but readers still rate this the best small hotel in town. This is one of the highest resorts in Austria but the straggling village lacks a heart. Just below the church is this hotel, built in 1958 and named for the 2095-metre mountain straight across the ravine.

'Another dark, rather old-fashioned interior' was our first impression. That refers to the entrance. 'Strikingly modern, Italian influence' was our reaction to the restaurant and bar. Glasses glitter against a mirror, reflecting light on to the white walls. In one room, cushions and curtains are in patterns of deep purple, black and red; in another, wooden chairs are painted peacock-blue. Even the menu covers are fuchsia. Only the white stove looks typically Austrian.

Guests, mainly from Italy and France, include families who are now bringing their grandchildren. No doubt they approve of the changes, such as the hyacinth-blue fabrics and bleached wood in some bedrooms, the wicker chairs and pale pink and lilac colours in others. What remains the same is the 2-minute run down through the woods to the Uga ski-lift.

Nearby Oberdamüls ski-lift, winter sports, hiking.

6884 Damüls
Tel (05510) 211
Fax (05510) 21120
Location on road in middle of Damüls; car parking outside, garage
Meals breakfast, lunch, dinner, snacks
Prices DB&B SS-SSS; reductions for children
Rooms 20 double; all have bath or shower, central heating, phone, TV radio
Facilities 2 dining-rooms, sitting-room, bar, terrace; sauna and solarium
Credit Cards AE, DC, MC, V
Children very welcome
Disabled not suitable
Pets accepted
Closed mid-Oct to early Dec; 4 weeks after Easter; restaurant only, Wed
Languages English, French, Italian
Proprietor Ingo Madlener

Vorarlberg

Bed-and-breakfast hotel, Feldkirch

Alpenrose

The enthusiasm we expressed for the Alpenrose in the first edition of this book has not diminished. If anything, it has increased. This is just the sort of hotel we always hope to find in a pretty old town but seldom do. Located in the pedestrian zone, at the end of a tiny cobbled passageway, roses climb along the front of the building which has been in the same family for generations. The current owner, Mrs. Gutwinski, is always making improvements and in 1994, she gave the entire hotel a facelift. What's more, she changed the room numbers, so regulars requesting a favourite room should double-check when booking.

In what is now number 30, yellow makes the room seem bright despite small windows while soft grey-blue gives it warmth. Number 21 has dainty ribbon-patterned wallpaper while number 9 has a tiny balcony. Bathrooms are on the small side but well thought-out, with large mirrors and adequate shelf space. Even the corridors are pleasant, with 19thC portraits and furniture. Reservations must be made well in advance of the June Schubertiade festival, when many rooms are taken by artists, and you may even hear singers and musicians practising.

Nearby cathedral, Katzenturm, Rathaus, Schattenburg castle.

6800 Feldkirch, Rosengasse 6
Tel (05522) 22175
Fax (05522) 221755
Location in pedestrian area in old town but access for guests allowed; own car parking
Meals breakfast, snacks
Prices rooms SS-SSSS with breakfast
Rooms 20 double, 5 single, 2 suites; all have bath or shower, central heating, phone, TV, minibar, hairdrier
Facilities 2 breakfast rooms, sitting-room
Credit Cards AE, DC, MC, V
Children welcome
Disabled easy access to Room 9; lift/elevator
Pets accepted
Closed never
Languages English, French, Italian
Proprietor Mrs. Rosi Gutwinski

Vorarlberg

❄ **Resort hotel, Gargellen** ❄

Alpenhotel Heimspitze

Set across the river from the village, the hotel has an atmosphere of seclusion, with a large garden and nothing but mountains behind. Originally a simple epension, it was rebuilt in 1969 in a traditional style but with modern spaciousness. The family like to collect: plenty of china, some pewter, and hundreds of ducks. That is Frau Thöny's hobby and she has examples from all over the world. There are even ducks in the sauna.

She has also chosen the furnishings for the bedrooms: oatmeal-coloured carpeting with woven rugs on top, a panel of fabric on a wall to match the curtains, and bed linen of pale pink, yellow, or blue. Even the single rooms are special, with painted furniture. And everyone finds flowers, chocolates or schnapps on arrival. There are two dining-rooms and a basement bar but the most popular room is the century-old, candle-lit *Maises-Stüble* with tiny wild-flower pictures and inlaid-wood tables. The award-winning kitchen produces home-made jams, *Stollen* and a choice of five or six different cakes plus a menu that changes daily. In summer, children climb on the adventure playground and look for frogs in the near-by pond.

Nearby winter sports, hiking.

6787 Gargellen
Tel (05557) 6319
Fax (05557) 631920
Location across bridge, on east side of valley; car parking outside and covered
Meals breakfast, lunch, dinner, snacks
Prices DB&B from SS-SSSS; reductions for children
Rooms 15 double, 3 single, 2 suites; all have bath or shower, central heating, phone; some hairdrier; TV on request
Facilities 2 dining-rooms, sitting-room, bar, terrace; sauna, massage, fitness area; playground, garden, curling
Credit Cards AE, DC, MC, V
Children very welcome
Disabled not suitable
Pets by request **Closed** mid-Oct to mid-Dec; mid-April to mid-June **Languages** English, French, Italian
Proprietors Thöny family

Vorarlberg

❄ Traditional chalet, Kleinwalsertal ❄

Sonnenberg

Every now and then we like a place so much we are tempted to keep it just for ourselves. This is it. Set high above the village of Hirschegg, the approach is up one of the steepest hills we have ever driven, or walked. When we arrived in summer, the garden was abloom with daisies, poppies, and iris. Kurt, from Germany, and Martine, from Alsace, take understandable delight in showing off their house, which dates back to 1530.

Ceilings are low and the ancient wood creaks with every step up to the bedrooms; each has a different colour scheme, but all have canopied four-poster beds plus bathrobes and walking sticks. Some hotel bedrooms are just for sleeping; these are comfortable enough to spend time in, though guests also relax in the basement sitting-room, where picture windows look straight across the valley. A small swimming-pool is like a grotto, built into a wall of rock.

Tables in the two snug dining-rooms are shared, so guests get to know one another over leisurely evening meals. Once a week there are gourmet suppers when the chef produces half-a-dozen courses of French, Italian or regional specialities.

Nearby winter sports, hiking.

6992 Hirschegg, Kleinwalsertal, Am Berg 26
Tel (05517) 5433
Fax (05517) 543333
Location on west side of valley above Hirschegg; car parking across street
Meals breakfast, dinner, snacks
Prices rooms MM-MMMM with breakfast
Rooms 16 double, 1 single, 2 suites; all have bath or shower, central heating, phone, TV, radio, hairdrier
Facilities dining-room, sitting-room, terrace; indoor swimming-pool; garden
Credit Cards not accepted
Children accepted
Disabled not suitable
Pets small dogs only
Closed Nov to mid-Dec; mid-Apr to mid-May
Languages English, French
Proprietors Krieger family

Vorarlberg

❄ Resort hotel, Kleinwalsertal ❄

Steinbock

Hans Vogler believes in having "a good life as well as a good business." He is from Allgäu, just over the German border, his wife is from the Bregenzerwald, and they spent years working in Sweden and the Benelux countries before buying a small guest-house here in 1981. Expansion and improvements have been made carefully; for example, the lower-level bar is so well-insulated that guests in the restaurant above cannot hear the music. Each bedroom comes with an umbrella and guests can use the washing-machine and tumble-drier in the basement. Furnishings throughout are solid and comfortable.

Breakfast is a feast. Cut your own slices of *Bio* (organic) breads and cheeses, scoop butter from its wooden tub and boil or fry an egg on the little table-stove. Cereals are stored in the drawers of an old cupboard, there are several bowls of dried and fresh fruits, and six types of tea. The Sunday barbecue is an institution; Herr Vogler presides, cooking *Bratwurst*, chicken and steaks while a band plays all the old favourites. Tall, with a handle-bar moustache, he enjoys playing 'mine host'. "My hobbies in winter are cross-country and downhill skiing ... and throwing snowballs."

Nearby winter sports, hiking, tennis.

6993 Mittelberg, Kleinwalsertal, Bödmerstr 46
Tel (05517) 5033
Fax (05517) 3164
Location in southernmost village of valley; ample car parking
Meals breakfast, lunch, dinner, snacks
Prices rooms MM-MMM with breakfast; reductions for children
Rooms 27 double, all have bath or shower, central heating, phone, TV, radio, minibar, safe
Facilities 2 dining-rooms, sitting-room, bar/disco; sauna, washing machine; terrace
Credit Cards not accepted
Children very welcome
Disabled not suitable
Pets accepted **Closed** Nov to mid-Dec; 2 weeks after Easter
Languages English, Swedish
Proprietors Vogler family

Vorarlberg

❄ **Restaurant with rooms, Kleinwalsertal** ❄

Almhof Rupp

Friedhelm Rupp has won acclaim and two *toques* from *Gault Millau* for his cuisine. As well as the superb à la carte menu, the half-board menu is impressive with dishes such as asparagus with smoked salmon strips, calves' liver with Madeira sauce, and rhubarb strudel. Each week a different gala menu is offered, with 6 or 7 courses of Italian, French or Austrian dishes. The wine list is as international as the food.

Built 30 years ago, this is no architectural gem, set just off the main road with the car park in front. The back overlooks a roaring mountain stream and the Kanzelwandbahn lift. Rooms are being renovated; out go the dark colours, in come panels of natural linen, white paint on the wood, and a carpet of cream and blue, creating an altogether lighter look. These have bright, white, roomy bathrooms with double wash-basins. In the bar, bench seats surround the circular open fireplace and look right into the restaurant. This retains the old-fashioned rustic look, with brown wood and orange curtains. Facing south, it is flooded with natural light in summer and lit by candles on winter evenings. Herr Rupp enjoys leading hiking tours in the summer.

Nearby winter sports, hiking.

6991 Riezlern, Kleinwalsertal
Tel (05517) 5004
Fax (05517) 3273
Location in middle of village; car parking outside, garage
Meals breakfast, dinner, snacks
Prices rooms MM-MMMM with breakfast; reductions for children
Rooms 28 double, 1 single; all have bath or shower; central heating, phone, TV, radio
Facilities 2 dining-rooms, bar, TV room, 2 games rooms, terrace; sauna, beauty treatment, small indoor pool
Credit Cards not accepted
Children very welcome
Disabled not suitable
Pets accepted; not in dining-room
Closed Nov to mid-Dec; after Easter to mid-May **Languages** English, some French, Italian
Proprietor Friedhelm Rupp

Vorarlberg

❄ **Old farmhouse, Kleinwalsertal** ❄

s'Breitachhus

In winter, this looks like an iced gingerbread house; in summer clematis, roses, and geraniums cover the front. Bought by Harald and Christine Riezler 20 years ago, the building dates back over 300 years and has the darkened wood to prove it. Step across the deep porch, bend your head through the tiny doorway and you are inside a private home. Like most, it is furnished with an eclectic mixture of old and new. Pictures of children are everywhere but pride of place is given to the blown-up wedding photograph of the Riezlers in traditional Kleinwalsertal dress, with Christine wearing the special crown and green apron of the Walser bride.

Bedrooms come in all shapes and sizes and are prettily, if simply, decorated. Two have four-poster beds; all have balconies and modern bathrooms. Harald's menu is good home-style cooking with a choice for vegetarians and at breakfast, jams and wholemeal rolls are home-made.

Guests get to know one another, talking in the little sitting-room with its warming oven and eating in the honey-coloured, wood-panelled dining-room. Smokers, however, are expected to go outside for a puff.

Nearby Parsenn ski-lift, winter sports, hiking.

6991 Riezlern, Kleinwalsertal, Eggstr 14
Tel (05517) 6266
Fax (05517) 6266107
Location on hillside above Riezlern; ample car parking
Meals breakfast, dinner, snacks
Prices rooms M-MMM with breakfast; in winter, DB&B only; reductions for children
Rooms 9 double, 1 single; all have bath or shower, central heating, phone; some TV, radio
Facilities dining-room, sitting-room, TV room, whirl-pool in cellar, terrace
Credit Cards not accepted
Children very welcome
Disabled not suitable
Pets not accepted **Closed** Nov to early Dec (snow); 2-4 weeks after Easter **Languages** some English, French
Proprietors Riezler family

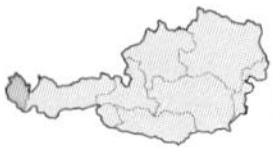

Vorarlberg

❄ **Old house, Kleinwalsertal** ❄

Walser Stuba

The village of Riezlern is named for this family, one of the original Walsers who left Switzerland some 600 years ago. The owners of the Breitachhus just up the hill are cousins. Not surprisingly, this is a traditional household.

In the 'Walser Marriage Gallery', the family tree on the wall dates back to the 16thC. A glass case displays the wedding crown, handed down through seven generations, along with the bridal dress. Once a week the family even gives a talk and slide show explaining the customs and history of the Kleinwalsertal.

Furnishings are exactly what is expected of a traditional country inn: enormous baskets of dried flowers, decorative carved wood and bench seating. Yet it was built in 1985, so most rooms are larger than in an old building and there is a glassed-in terrace next to the dining-room. Local game features on the menu, but a vegetarian dish is also offered and older folk can ask for smaller portions. At the other end of the age range, colouring pencils are provided so tiny children can draw on their special menus. The resident 'babysitter' is Laura, a noisy, yellow and blue parrot who does acrobatic tricks on her swing and shows off constantly.

Nearby Parsenn ski-lift, winter sports, hiking.

6991 Riezlern, Kleinwalsertal
Tel (05517) 53460
Fax (05517) 534613
Location on hillside above village of Riezlern; car parking outside
Meals breakfast, lunch, dinner, snacks
Prices DB&B MM-MMMM with breakfast; reductions for children
Rooms 20 double, 4 single; all have bath or shower, central heating, phone, TV, hairdrier, radio, safe
Facilities 3 dining-rooms, sitting-room, bar, terrace; fitness and health area; babysitting
Credit Cards AE, DC, MC, V
Children very welcome
Disabled some access
Pets accepted **Closed** Nov to mid-Dec; restaurant only, Tues
Languages English
Proprietors Riezler family

Vorarlberg

❄ **Resort hotel, Lech am Arlberg** ❄

Silencehotel Angela

Many hotels promise great comfort and a 'home from home' ambience; few achieve both. This one does. "If guests want to have breakfast at noon, they can have it," says Luise Walch who, with her husband, Elmar, transformed this old farmhouse.

They kept the back door, cracked with age, and put it behind the reception desk, along with a trumpeting angel and a big bell. There are, however, none of the rustic bits and pieces which all too often create a contrived and cluttered look.

Rooms are named for the mountain in view and all have different fabrics, from tartans to florals. The 'small' ones are far from cramped, while the new suites are handsome, with bold patterns standing out against a white and cream background. The penthouse has a kitchen and a maid will come in to cook breakfast. Dinner in the pink and pine-green dining-room runs to six courses.

Just above the village, the hotel is surrounded by meadows full of gentian and cows. Herr Walch is a local and leads walking tours; as a former head of the ski school he can advise on the best places to ski, starting right from the door.

Nearby Schlegelkopf lift, winter sports, hiking.

6764 Lech am Arlberg, 62
Tel (05583) 2407
Fax (05583) 240715
Location up twisting road on hillside above town; ample car parking; indoor garage
Meals breakfast, lunch, dinner snacks
Prices rooms SS-SSSS with breakfast; in winter, DB&B only; reductions for children
Rooms 28 double, 2 single; all have bath or shower, central heating, phone, TV, minibar, radio, safe
Facilities dining-room, sitting-room, bar, games-room, terrace; large health and fitness area
Credit Cards not accepted
Children very welcome
Disabled not suitable
Pets not accepted **Closed** Oct, Nov; May, June **Languages** English, French, Italian
Proprietors Walch family

Vorarlberg

❄ **Modern hotel, Lech-Zug** ❄

Hotel Rote Wand

Our inspector found no greater contrast between old and new anywhere else in Austria. Josef Walch Jr's restaurant is as traditional as you can get and famous for fondues. The hotel provides 'the shock of the new'. Colours are fresh turquoise and green, soft lilac and violet, set off by white walls and the palest of wood. Fabrics are checks and plaids. Even the basics are turned into features: stair railings are painted aquamarine while upright radiators look like organ pipes. Bedrooms are straight out of a design magazine with custom-made furniture and beds are upstairs in the split-level galleries.

The emphasis is on health and fitness. Photographs of Jane Fonda-types adorn the reception area and there is a wide choice of exercise programmes, from aerobics and jogging to water gymnastics and weight training. In winter, anyone opting out of skiing can practice golf shots in the basement driving range or play tennis on the nearby indoor courts. Children, too, are well-catered for. There is a large swimming-pool, an outdoor playground and a first-rate indoor playroom, with a resident nanny during the main holiday season.

Nearby winter sports, hiking, tennis.

6764 Lech-Zug am Arlberg
Tel (05583) 34350
Fax (05583) 343540
Location in hamlet of Zug, near Lech; car parking outside
Meals breakfast, lunch, dinner, snacks
Prices DB&B SSS-SSSS; children under 6 free
Rooms 34 double, all have bath and shower, central heating, phone, TV, minibar, hairdrier
Facilities 3 dining-rooms, sitting-room, bar, terrace; games-rooms, billiard table, indoor swimming pool
Credit Cards AE, DC
Children very welcome
Disabled very good access; lift/elevator
Pets accepted
Closed Nov to early Dec; mid-April to early June **Languages** English, French, Italian
Proprietors Josef Walch family

Vorarlberg

❄ Restaurant with rooms, Schruns ❄

Hotel Krone

On our first visit, the bedrooms struck as looking rather bland, as if Robert Mayer had channeled all his creativity into cooking, rather than room decoration. Our readers, however, disagree, describing them as 'pleasantly formal and old-fashioned, rather like the owner'.

There is no doubt that Robert Mayer is an above-average chef with one of the finest restaurants in the Montafon valley. As well as the traditional *Tafelspitz* (boiled beef), Mayer nods towards France when he delicately sauces *ris-de-veau* and poaches salmon and zander in garlic and tomato butter. The *Montafonstube*, with its caramel-coloured, heavily-knotted pine panelling is a 'must' for visitors. The windows are leaded and the octagonal tables are inlaid with slates, which was used both as a stand for hot pans and as a chalk-board for farmers doing business on market-day.

Upstairs, the ceiling of the *Kronestube* is painted with signs of the zodiac. The terrace garden is a plus, as is the location - just a few steps from the middle of the lovely old part of Schruns. Forget the arguments about room decoration, for convenience, history and food, this old tavern makes a fine place to stay.

Nearby old town; Montafon ski area, winter sports, hiking.

6780 Schruns
Tel (05556) 72255
Fax (05556) 74879
Location near middle of town, next to river; car parking across the street
Meals breakfast, lunch, dinner, snacks
Prices rooms S-SS with breakfast; reductions for children
Rooms 8 double, 1 single; all have bath or shower, central heating, phone, minibar, radio; TV on request
Facilities 2 dining-rooms, sitting-room, terrace
Credit Cards DC
Children welcome but not suitable
Disabled not suitable
Pets accepted **Closed** mid-Oct to mid-Dec; after Easter to early June **Languages** English, French, some Italian
Proprietors Mayer family

Vorarlberg

❄ Old inn, Schwarzenberg ❄

Romantik Hotel Hirschen

You can't miss this 18thC inn, opposite the church on the main crossroads in the village. The whole of Schwarzenberg is a national treasure, with its wooden-shingled houses so typical of the Bregenzerwald valley. Few hotels succeed in being all things to all people but the Fetz family, who have been here for 100 years, manage to do just that. Locals pop in for a drink in the low-ceilinged *Jägerstube* but for special occasions book into the restaurant, rated one of the best in the area.

Families arrive in winter for ski holidays but during the summer the hotel is filled with couples. There is even a choice of style in bedrooms. The old house is traditional and romantic, either with Louis Philippe-style furniture or Laura Ashley prints. Rooms are larger in the modern annexe, with more of a country look. Colours here are delicate shades of purple, blue, and green, with touches of bright pink or yellow. This is also where small business seminars are held, away from other guests.

Behind the village, the Hochälpelekopf is covered with ski runs; cross-country trails loop round the valley.

Nearby Angelika Kaufmann paintings, altar-piece in baroque church; local museum.

6867 Schwarzenberg
Tel (05512) 29440
Fax (05512) 294420
Location in middle of old village; ample car parking, underground garage
Meals breakfast, lunch, dinner, snacks
Prices rooms SS-SSSS with breakfast; reductions for children
Rooms 14 double, 10 single, 6 suites; all have bath or shower, central heating, phone, TV, minibar, hairdrier; some radio,**Facilities** 3 dining-rooms, sitting-room, *Stube*, seminar rooms, sauna, terrace
Credit Cards AE, DC, MC, V
Children welcome **Disabled** not suitable **Pets** accepted
Closed never; restaurant only, Wed, Thurs lunch (except summer) **Languages** English, French, Italian
Proprietors Fetz family

Vorarlberg

❄ **Mountain lodge, Silbertal** ❄

Gasthof Kristberg

When everyone else has gone down to the valley and the cable car has stopped for the night, guests at this simple inn have the mountain to themselves. There are few other buildings on this slope high above Silbertal and just 100 m from the top of the Kristbergbahn. Herr Zudrell, his wife and grown-up children welcome guests and run the kitchen. Everything from eggs to meat comes from local farms. At the entrance, a display case overflows with their children's ski trophies. The atmosphere is more 'home' than 'hotel'. Bedrooms in the new wing are cheerful, with a teddy-bear pattern on children's duvets; the few old rooms with shared bath and lavatory facilities are ideal for groups of friends or families who appreciate a bargain.

"You have to want to be with other people," one of the daughters, told us in her excellent English. Guests spend time talking after dinner, there are games for children, and sometimes a torch-lit evening walk in winter. In summer, farmers in green boots congregate at the *Stammtisch* and walkers stop for cold drinks. Informality is the rule; this is not for anyone wearing designer clothes and expecting five-star service.

Nearby winter sports, hiking trails, Kristbergbahn

6780 Silbertal, Kristberg 240
Tel (05556) 72290
Fax (05556) 722905
Location above Silbertal valley; phone ahead for access by car; otherwise 5 minutes' walk from cable car
Meals breakfast, lunch, dinner, snacks
Prices rooms S-SSS with breakfast
Rooms 12 double, 3 single, 1 separate cabin; all have central heating, phone; most have bath or shower; TV on request
Facilities dining-room, sitting-room, bar, TV room, terrace; small gymnasium
Credit Cards not accepted
Children very welcome
Disabled not suitable
Pets accepted
Closed Nov to mid-Dec; 1 week after Easter; 3 weeks May
Languages English, French
Proprietors Zudrell family

Vorarlberg

❄ Bed-and-breakfast hotel, Au ❄

Haus Alpina

More like a home than a hotel. Some bedrooms have traditional painted furniture, others are modern, but all have up-to-date bathrooms. Fitness area in the basement and cross-country skiing from the door through surrounding meadows.

■ 6883 Au, Rehmen 30 **Tel** (05515) 2365 **Fax** (05515) 236571 **Meals** breakfast **Prices** rooms S-SS with breakfast **Rooms** 16, all with shower, central heating, phone **Credit Cards** not accepted **Closed** Nov to mid-Dec **Languages** French

❄ Old inn, Bezau ❄

Gasthof Sonne

On the edge of a pretty Bregenzerwald village, this clever blend of old and new has painted shutters and window-boxes of red geraniums facing the road. Behind is an extension with games rooms plus health and fitness spa. Good cross-country skiing.

■ 6870 Bezau **Tel** (05514) 2262 or 2470 **Fax** (05514) 2912 **Meals** breakfast, lunch, dinner, snacks **Prices** rooms S-SS with breakfast **Rooms** 30, all with bath or shower, central heating, phone, TV, radio **Credit Cards** not accepted **Closed** Nov **Languages** English

Old inn, Braz bei Bludenz

Gasthof Rössle

The Bargehr family have given a facelift to this inn, located next to the church. Fresh paint outside and attractive rustic-style bedrooms inside. A good base for Klostertal skiers and the imaginative menus are also attracting attention.

■ 6751 Braz bei Bludenz, Arlbergstr 67 **Tel** (05552) 8105 **Fax** (05552) 81056 **Meals** breakfast, lunch, dinner **Prices** rooms S-SS with breakfast **Rooms** 10, all with bath or shower, central heating, phone; TV by request **Credit Cards** DC, MC, V **Closed** 2 weeks June; 2 weeks Dec; restaurant only, Mon, Tues lunch **Languages** English, French, Spanish

❄ Old inn, Braz bei Bludenz ❄

Gasthof Traube Braz

In winter, skiers head for the Sonnenkopf in the Klostertal; in summer, golfers play on the new Bludenz-Braz course nearby. Also recommended for families with young children. Plain bedrooms, attractive public rooms, plus ambitious menus.

■ 6751 Braz bei Bludenz, Klostertalestr **Tel** (05552) 8103 **Fax** (05552) 810340 **Meals** breakfast, lunch, dinner, snacks **Prices** rooms S-SSS with breakfast **Rooms** 22, with bath or shower, central heating, phone, radio **Credit Cards** MC, V **Closed** Nov **Languages** English, French, Italian, Spanish

Vorarlberg

Mountain hotel, Eichenberg bei Bregenz

Hotel Schönblick

Worth staying for the breathtaking views across Lake Constance. The terrace of this 1980s hotel attracts tourists and locals alike but the Hehle family also have a fine restaurant, adequate bedrooms, indoor swimming-pool with sauna, tennis courts.

■ 6911 Eichenberg bei Bregenz **Tel** (05574) 45965 **Fax** (05574) 459657 **Meals** breakfast, lunch, dinner, snacks **Prices** rooms S-SSS with breakfast **Rooms** 22, all with bath or shower, central heating, phone, TV; some with minibar **Credit Cards** not accepted **Closed** mid-Nov to mid-Dec; early Jan to early Feb **Languages** English, French

❄ Chalet hotel, Damüls ❄

Berghotel Madlener

High in the Bregenzerwald and just out of the village, this is a first-rate example of a new hotel built in the familiar chalet style. Ceilings and walls are panelled in pale wood, logs blaze in corner fireplaces, bedrooms are bright with flowery fabrics.

■ 6884 Damüls, Haus 22 **Tel** (05510) 2210 **Fax** (05510) 22115 **Meals** breakfast, lunch, dinner, snacks **Prices** rooms S-SS with breakfast **Rooms** 26, all with bath or shower, central heating, phone; TV on request **Credit Cards** not accepted **Closed** Nov **Languages** English

❄ Mountain resort hotel, Gaschurn ❄

Landhotel Älpili

There are two Älpilis on the edge of town, the old barn-turned-restaurant and the new luxury hotel next door. Furnishings are striking: pale pink, green and white for the bedrooms (all large), and bold green and purple for the dining room.

■ 6793 Gaschurn **Tel** (05558) 87330 **Fax** (05558) 873371 **Meals** breakfast, lunch, dinner, snacks **Prices** rooms S-SSSS with breakfast **Rooms** 19, all with bath and shower, central heating, phone, TV, minibar **Credit Cards** not accepted **Closed** mid-Oct to mid-Dec; after Easter to mid-May **Languages** English

❄ Resort village hotel, Gaschurn ❄

Hotel Monika

Monika Bergauer refurbished her hotel 12 years ago, keeping the golden pine panelling but adding soft blue fabrics to the dining-room. Bedrooms remain cramped. Indoor health spa, outdoor swimming-pool; 100 m from Silvretta Nova gondola.

■ 6793 Gaschurn **Tel** (05558) 82910 **Fax** (05558) 8126 **Meals** breakfast, dinner **Prices** rooms S-SSSS with breakfast **Rooms** 24, all with bath or shower, central heating, phone, TV, minibar **Credit Cards** AE, DC, MC, V **Closed** May, Nov **Languages** English

Vorarlberg

❄ Mountain resort hotel, Gaschurn ❄

Hotel Saladina

Only a minute's walk from the Versettla gondola station, the Wohlesers' inn has a gloomy outside but a cheery interior, lightened by large windows and honey-coloured pine. The sauna, whirlpool and outdoor swimming-pool are a bonus.

■ 6793 Gaschurn **Tel** (05558) 8204 **Fax** (05558) 820421 **Meals** breakfast, lunch, dinner, snacks **Prices** rooms S-SSS with breakfast **Rooms** 15 rooms, all with bath or shower, central heating, phone, TV, radio, minibar **Credit Cards** not accepted **Closed** Nov to mid-Dec **Languages** English

❄ Town hotel, Kleinwalsertal ❄

Hotel Jagdhof

Recently-expanded, this central meeting place is across from the casino. No wonder breakfast is served until noon. Bedrooms are quiet, with balconies and plenty of storage space. There is a fine health and fitness spa, plus a heated outdoor swimming-pool.

■ 6991 Riezlern, Walserstr 27 **Tel** (05517) 5603 **Fax** (05517) 3348 (code from Germany 08329) **Meals** breakfast, lunch, dinner **Prices** rooms MM-MMMM **Rooms** 45, all with bath or shower, central heating, phone, TV **Credit Cards** MC **Closed** never **Languages** English, French

❄ Mountain resort hotel, Lech am Arlberg ❄

Brunnenhof

The highlight here is the cooking of Master chef Balthasar Thaler. His wife, Angelika, runs this fashionable hotel, which is open only in the winter. Pale carved wood, dried flowers, and subtle fabrics are artfully combined. Expensive.

■ 6764 Lech am Arlberg **Tel** (05583) 2349 **Fax** (05583) 234959 **Meals** breakfast, lunch, dinner, snacks **Prices** rooms SSS-SSSS with breakfast **Rooms** 21, all with bath or shower, central heating, phone, TV, radio, safe **Credit Cards** AE, DC **Closed** May to Nov; restaurant only, Sun **Languages** English, French

❄ Resort hotel, Lech am Arlberg ❄

Hotel Haldenhof

Daily European newspapers and international dishes on the menu reflect the regular clientele. Heavy brown timbers, autumnal colours and thick rugs on quarry tile floors create a warmth matched by the Schwärzlers' welcome. Near ski school.

■ 6764 Lech am Arlberg **Tel** (05583) 24440 **Fax** (05583) 244421 **Meals** breakfast, lunch, dinner, snacks **Prices** rooms S-SSSS **Rooms** 22, all with bath or shower, central heating, phone, TV, radio, hairdrier **Credit Cards** AE, MC, V **Closed** May, June; mid-Sept to early Dec **Languages** English, French, Italian

Vorarlberg

❄ Mountain resort hotel, Lech am Arlberg ❄

Hotel Madlochblick

Understandably popular thanks to steady upgrading of facilities. There are cheerful sitting areas with lots of wood, deep chairs and open fireplaces. Bedrooms are decorated in neutral beige. More suited to adults than families. Well-planned fitness area.

■ 6764 Lech am Arlberg **Tel** (05583) 2220 **Fax** (05583) 3416 **Meals** breakfast, lunch, dinner, snacks **Prices** rooms S-SSSS, with breakfast **Rooms** 25, all with bath, central heating, phone, TV, radio, hair-drier, safe **Credit Cards** not accepted **Closed** 20 Sept to early Dec; end April to early July **Languages** English

Restaurant with rooms, Rankweil

Gasthof Mohren

Roland Hofer's cooking is the attraction here. Menus include both traditional Vorarlberg specialities and lighter dishes. Modern, practical and comfortable rooms. A good base for touring and for Bregenz and Feldkirch music festivals.

■ 6830 Rankweil, Stiegstr 17 **Tel** (05522) 44275 **Fax** (05522) 442755 **Meals** breakfast, lunch, dinner, snacks **Prices** rooms S-SSS with breakfast **Rooms** 15, all with bath or shower, central heating, phone, TV, radio **Credit Cards** DC, MC, V **Closed** restaurant only, Mon **Languages** English

❄ Chalet hotel, Warth am Arlberg ❄

Hotel Lechtaler Hof

The Brenner's hotel may be small, but the rooms are certainly comfortable, with deep balconies to soak up the sun. First-class spa and fitness area. Special adventure holidays for horse-lovers, walkers, mountain bikers. Ski-school next to the hotel.

■ 6767 Warth am Arlberg **Tel** (05583) 2677 **Fax** (05583) 36868 **Meals** breakfast, lunch, dinner, snacks **Prices** rooms S-SSS with breakfast **Rooms** 15, all with bath or shower, central heating, TV, radio, mini-bar **Credit Cards** not accepted **Closed** Oct to early Dec; after Easter to early May **Languages** English, French, Italian

❄ Mountain resort hotel, Warth am Arlberg ❄

s'Walserberg Hotel

Warth is a remote village high in the mountains, so the Walch family provide a lot for guests, from a café and pizzeria to a bakery and hairdresser. Ski from the door in winter; learn to paint in summer. Simple comforts, good for families.

■ 6767 Warth am Arlberg **Tel** (05583) 35020 **Fax** (05583) 344122 **Meals** breakfast, lunch, dinner, snacks **Prices** rooms S-SSS with breakfast **Rooms** 29, all with bath or shower, central heating, phone, TV **Credit Cards** not accepted **Closed** Nov to mid-Dec; after Easter to June **Languages** English

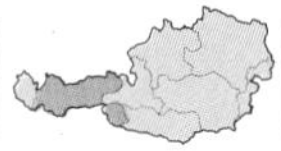

Tirol

Area introduction

Hotels in the Tyrol

The Tyrol (Tirol in German) must be Austria's most famous region around the world, thanks to spectacular scenery, excellent skiing and photogenic villages. It also boasts a turbulent history, reflected in the state's hymn, dedicated to one Andreas Hofer. A resistance fighter in the early 19thC, his name crops up everywhere in recognition of his battles with the Bavarians and Napoleon. The region's riches have always attracted neighbouring nations, and, after the First World War, a large chunk of Tyrol was ceded to Italy, which is still referred to as South Tyrol today.

Statistics show that this most touristy region is also the least-populated, proving that there are many peaceful and pretty corners to be found where buses never pass.

As our inspectors found many hotels that relied on the constant stream of tours, they were particularly pleased to find hoteliers who ignored the 'fast buck', preferring the time-honoured high standards set by their forefathers for decades. One or two are in the very heart of Innsbruck or Igls, others at the end of remote valleys or on picturesque lakes: all set standards that many fellow-Tiroleans find hard to match.

As well as Baroque churches with onion domes, medieval villages and atmospheric towns, the Tyroleans hold brass bands dear to their hearts. They also love to have good time, and tend to welcome visitors into any party they are throwing.

East Tyrol is a fragment of the Federal State that was cut off when South Tyrol was ceded to Italy in 1919. Lienz, a busy small town, is the focal point at the meeting of the Isel and Drau Rivers, but there is an air of yesteryear about this small island to the north of the Dolomites, where tourists are less numerous than in the rest of Tyrol.

For further details of the area, contact:
Tirol Werbung,
Tyrol Tourist Board,
Maria-Theresien-Strasse 55,
A-6010 Innsbruck
Tel (0512) 5320170
Fax (0512) 5320174

This page acts as an introduction to the features of Tyrol. The long entries for this state - covering the hotels we are most enthusiastic about - start on the next page. But do not neglect the shorter entries starting on page 57: these are all hotels where we would happily stay.

Tirol

❄ **Old chalet hotel, Ehrwald** ❄

Hotel Spielmann

Staying here is like staying with Austrian friends. The hotel is an old Tyrolean house, run as a hotel by a family that dates back to the 1600s. Spielmann father and son are a rare combination: both are well-known mountain climbers as well as first-class chefs. Set on the edge of the village and away from traffic, the traditionally-painted house is surrounded by meadows. Some rooms have dark wood, others have pale, but all, even the singles, have a balcony. Colour is added by fresh and dried flowers, straw dolls and the family collection of 19thC Tyrolean prints.

The restaurant has a sound reputation and features recipes from grandma's cookbook; ingredients such as herbs, lamb and home-smoked *Speck* come from their own farm. Home-made breads and jams await breakfasters and once a week, out come zither and guitar, "not because we have to but because *Stubenmusik* was played here long before tourism began." Children love the spotlessly-clean barns, playground and swimming-pool; parents are thankful for the washing-machine. Best of all is hiking with the Spielmanns, perhaps to spot game, eagles and wild-flowers; or, in winter, climbing fresh snow on seal-skins.

Nearby Sonnenhang ski-lifts, ski-school; cross-country trails.

6632 Ehrwald
Tel (05673) 22250
Fax (05673) 22255
Location in meadows outside village; ample car parking
Meals breakfast, lunch, dinner, snacks
Prices rooms SS-SSS with breakfast; reductions for children
Rooms 18 double, 4 single, 4 suites, 4 apartments; all have bath or shower, central heating, phone, TV, radio, safe **Facilities** 2 dining-rooms, sitting-room, bar, 2 TV rooms, games-room; terrace, garden, heated outdoor swimming-pool **Credit Cards** AE, DC, MC, V **Children** very welcome **Disabled** not suitable **Pets** accepted **Closed** Nov to mid-Dec; after Easter to late May **Languages** English, French, Italian
Proprietors Spielmann family

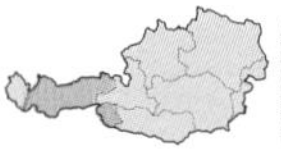

Tirol

❄ Country inn, Gnadenwald ❄

Gasthof Michaelerhof

Even from the road we reckoned this would make a good place to stay and closer inspection proved us right. The Schiestls took over this farmhouse in 1965, turning it first into a restaurant, then a hotel. Louis Schiestl worked as a chef all over the world, in Istanbul and Nairobi, Japan and Sweden before settling in this tiny hamlet and marrying a local woman.

Proof of his confidence is his 'open kitchen', visible through windows in the bar and the doorway opposite reception. Menus reflect his international career, with *Nasi goreng* from Indonesia, curry from India and smoked fish from Scandinavia alongside the familiar *Schnitzel* and *Tafelspitz*.

Similarly, animal skins from Africa lend an exotic touch to the traditional Austrian interior. Instead of one main restaurant, there are four little *Stuben*: one has a collection of wooden bowls, another French windows that open to the patio in summer. Only 10 minutes' drive from the middle of Innsbruck, this is as popular for Sunday lunch as it is for business visitors during the week. Bedrooms are comfortable if unexceptional. There are tennis courts, a playground and trails in the forest.

Nearby winter sports, hiking, mountaineering, riding.

6060 Gnadenwald
Tel (05223) 48128
Fax (05223) 481284
Location on plateau near Innsbruck; own car parking
Meals breakfast, lunch, dinner, snacks
Prices rooms S-SS with breakfast; reductions for children
Rooms 10 double, 2 single; all have bath or shower, central heating, phone; TV on request
Facilities 4 dining-rooms, sitting-room with TV, bar; terrace, tennis courts
Credit Cards AE, DC
Children very welcome
Disabled not suitable
Pets accepted
Closed late Nov to early Dec; early Jan to early Feb; early June to early July; restaurant only, Mon, Tues **Languages** English, some French, Italian
Proprietors Schiestl family

Tirol

❄ Lakeside hotel, Heiterwang ❄

Fischer Am See

Our hearts sank when we saw a camping and caravan site near this inn. Fortunately, it proved to be less intrusive that we feared. Apparently, some children like to sleep in a tent while their parents take bedrooms in the hotel. These are above-average in size, with comfortable beds and small but adequate bathrooms.

Downstairs, a jolly line of red, black and white-striped socks hangs over the reception area. Like the bedrooms, the dining rooms are practical rather than pretty, though on our visit, vases of wildflowers brightened each table and an old rowing boat served as an unusual buffet-table for breakfast in the mornings and for salads in the evening. Views of trees, mountains and water fill the modern picture windows.

Below the terrace is a landing stage for launches that shuttle up and down the interconnecting lakes of Heiterwangsee and Plansee. No petrol engines are allowed, so fishing, canoeing and rowing are unspoilt; but at this altitude (1,000 m) the water is warm enough for swimming only in July and August. In winter, moon-lit cross-country skiing excursions on the lake finish with steaming *Glühwein* at the bar.

Nearby lake, fishing, rowing, hiking, winter sports.

6611 Heiterwang
Tel (05674) 5116
Location at end of lane, facing lake; ample car parking
Meals breakfast, lunch, dinner, snacks
Prices rooms S-SS with breakfast; reductions for children
Rooms 8 double, 3 single; all have bath or shower, central heating
Facilities 3 dining-rooms, sitting-room, bar, sauna, solarium
Credit Cards not accepted
Children very welcome
Disabled not suitable
Pets accepted
Closed mid-Oct to mid-Dec; last 2 weeks Jan
Languages English, some French, Italian
Proprietors Bunte family

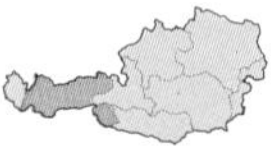

Tirol

❄ Castle hotel, Igls ❄

Schlosshotel Igls

Despite its prices, this remains a special treat, according to our readers. The new Lubinus suite would please the most fastidious Hollywood star, with two bathrooms and its own steam room. All bedrooms, however, combine what the owner describes as "the best from Italy and England, Spain and Austria." In less skilled hands that Euro-combination could spell disaster; luckily Frau Beck has the innate talent of a top interior designer. Every corner of this hundred-year-old villa is used, with architectural oddities turned into features; an octagonal turret, for example, becomes a little pine-panelled sitting-room.

There is a place for every mood. The blue and gold drawing room is formal with high ceilings and antiques; the bar has an open fire and leather armchairs. Downstairs, the restaurant reminded our inspector of a ship's dining-room, with curving walls and dark wood panelling. The swimming-pool is equally luxurious and, at the push of a button, a wall of glass disappears into the ground so swimmers can walk out into the garden. Close enough to Innsbruck for businessmen, there are golf courses and ski areas nearby. 'Outstanding' was the final verdict.

Nearby skiing, winter sports, golf, tennis

6080 Igls
Tel (0512) 377217
Fax (0512) 378679
Location on edge of village in own park; car parking outside, some under cover
Meals breakfast, lunch, dinner, snacks
Prices rooms SSSS; reductions for children
Rooms 10 double, 4 single, 6 suites; all have bath or shower, central heating, phone, TV, radio, minibar, hairdrier
Facilities 2 dining-rooms, sitting-room, bar, large gymnasium, indoor swimming-pool; terrace, garden
Credit Cards AE, DC, MC, V
Children welcome
Disabled access, lift/elevator
Pets accepted
Closed Nov to mid-Dec; 4 weeks after Easter **Languages** English, French, Italian
Proprietors Beck family

Tirol

❄ **Coaching inn, Imst** ❄

Hotel Post

Christa Pfeifer is the driving force behind the success of what was once Sprengenstein Castle. The old building, with its red and white chevrons on the shutters, seems steeped in history. Reception is at the top of the stairs, where the long, white corridor has a decorated ceiling and a gilded, wrought-iron gate. Antique chests of drawers, tables with huge vases of flowers, armchairs and mirrors create an ambience that is grand without being imposing.

Photographs do not do justice to the main dining-room. Not only are the wood panels dense with hand-carved trees and leaves, there is also a collection of the hideous masks for which the town is famous. The *Schemenlauf* (parade of spirits) takes place at Shrovetide every four years right outside the hotel. Every summer, however, guests sit out on the extraordinary covered terrace, decked with vines and flowers.

Bedrooms are handsome, with highly-polished wood and plush Edwardian-style fabrics; bathrooms, however, are right up-to-date. A large garden and enormous indoor swimming-pool are an added bonus.

Nearby skiing, winter sports, hiking, tennis, squash, rafting, mountaineering, fishing; SOS Children's Village

6460 Imst
Tel (05412) 66554
Fax (05412) 6651955
Location in heart of village in own park; ample car parking
Meals breakfast, lunch, dinner, snacks
Prices rooms SS-SSS with breakfast; reductions for children
Rooms 13 double, 10 suites, 3 single; all have bath or shower, central heating, phone, TV; some minibar, hairdrier
Facilities 2 dining-rooms, sitting-room, conference room, terrace; garden, indoor swimming-pool
Credit Cards AE, DC, MC, V
Children very welcome
Disabled not suitable
Pets accepted
Closed Nov to 1 Feb (approx)
Languages English, French, Italian
Proprietors Pfeifer family

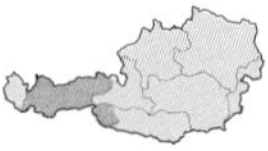

Tirol

❄ **Guest house, Innsbruck** ❄

Weisses Rössl

Popular tourist spots are all too often short of hotels that are right for this guide. This one is all but perfect. Find it right in the middle of the medieval old town. Climb the wide, tiled staircase to the restaurant one floor up and you will meet Werner Plank, wrapped in a long white apron, moving among the happy eaters, his voice booming above their conversations.

Originally owned by his grandfather, hard times forced his father to sell this 600 year-old inn. Young Werner worked his way around the world, saving up to re-install the Planks at the sign of the White Horse. In 1983, he succeeded. Since then he has completely renovated the medieval building: rewiring, replumbing and exposing the 16thC beams. Redecoration, with modern colours and furniture is sympathetic. The comfortable bedrooms have high ceilings, plain walls and soft blue curtains at the large windows. The restaurant is a meeting place for locals, who pop in for a chat and a game of cards. "They never look at the menu, just order the special of the day," whether it is home-made pasta, potato pancakes or strudel. Breakfast in the old *Stube*, hung with Tyrolean paintings, or on the quiet terrace.

Nearby Goldenes Dachl, Olympic Museum, cathedral, Hofburg.

6020 Innsbruck, Kiebachgasse 8 in der Altstadt
Tel (0512) 583057
Fax (0512) 5830575
Location in heart of old town, semi-pedestrian zone; public car parking nearby
Meals breakfast, lunch, dinner, snacks
Prices rooms SS-SSS with breakfast; reductions for children
Rooms 14 double; all have bath or shower, central heating, phone, radio, TV, hairdrier
Facilities 3 dining-rooms, terrace
Credit Cards AE, MC, V
Children welcome
Disabled reasonable access; lift/elevator **Pets** accepted
Closed 2 weeks Nov; 2 weeks after Easter **Languages** English, French, Italian
Proprietors Plank family

Tirol

❄ Mountain hotel, Kals ❄

Nationalpark-Hotel Taurerwirt

Although the Rogl family expanded their hotel, building an annexe in 1993, our readers tell us that, in this case, bigger is better. The bedrooms are more comfortable and the health and fitness spa is a welcome addition. Even the name has been changed to emphasize the stunning location at the head of a valley on the southern slopes of the Grossglockner. The approach road is twisting and steep, past gushing waterfalls, isolated chapels and the meadow where *Heidi* was filmed.

In summer, the silence is broken only by rushing streams and squeaking swallows. Children have a real adventure playground in the pine trees, while adults hike in the mountains and fish the rivers. Winter brings skiers, since the ski-school, ski kindergarten and half a dozen lifts are right outside the door, as are numerous cross-country trails. On our first visit, we were impressed by the enthusiasm of the Rogls and they are justifiably proud of their environmentally-friendly improvements. The restaurant serves up hearty portions and, with the old family farm next door, the chef is never short of fresh ingredients. We recommend this for anyone who enjoys Austria's great outdoors.

Nearby Glocknerblick lift, hiking, fishing, tennis.

9981 Kals am Grossglockner
Tel (04876) 226
Fax (04876) 22611
Location the last hotel at head of valley, surrounded by meadows; ample car parking
Meals breakfast, lunch, dinner, snacks
Prices DB&B S-SSS
Rooms 35 double: all have bath or shower, central heating, phone, radio; most with TV
Facilities dining-room, sitting-room, bar, TV room, non-smoking conservatory, terrace; garden; sauna, play-room, tennis courts, heated swimming-pool
Credit Cards not accepted
Children very welcome
Disabled some access
Pets accepted **Closed** mid-Oct to mid-Dec; after Easter to mid-May **Languages** English
Proprietors Rogl family

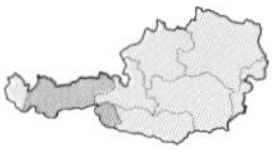

Tirol

❄ **Restaurant with rooms, Kufstein** ❄

Hotel Restaurant Alpenrose

Kufstein is famous for its Riedel glass factory and, fans would say, the nearby Alpenrose restaurant. The Telser brothers took over their parents' modest guest-house 20 years ago and built an international reputation for food.

Although Manfred has left, the restaurant continues to collect awards and is still considered 'the best place in town'. There are several major companies nearby and this is where the executives come to do business, so the sober, masculine atmosphere of the main dining-room is no surprise. Dark wood and brass are softened by gold fabrics; candles gleam against Riedel glassware. Tables in secluded corners are, no doubt, reserved for private conversations. The impressive wine list catalogues some 200 wines from France and Italy as well as Austria itself.

Thankfully, Johann Telser has not rested on his laurels. In 1996, bedrooms were given a much-needed overhaul, while the new suite comes with its own fireplace and sun terrace. The conference, fitness and spa facilities have also been upgraded. At breakfast, the *Bio-Ecke*, the healthy corner, encourages guests to start the day with muesli, natural yoghurt and juices.

Nearby Riedel glass factory, winter sports, hiking.

6330 Kufstein, Weissachstr 47
Tel (05372) 62122
Fax (05372) 621227
Location in quiet back street on edge of town; ample car parking, garage
Meals breakfast, lunch, dinner, snacks
Prices rooms SS-SSSS with breakfast; reductions for children
Rooms 17 double, 4 single; 1 suite; all have bath or shower, central heating, phone, TV, minibar; some safes
Facilities 3 dining-rooms, 2 sitting-rooms, TV room, conference room, sauna, solarium; garden
Credit Cards AE, MC
Children welcome **Disabled** easy access; lift/elevator **Pets** accepted **Closed** Palm Sunday to Easter **Languages** English, French, Italian
Proprietor Johann Telser

Tirol

❄ **Lakeside hotel, near Lienz** ❄

Parkhotel Tristachersee

Rules are made to be broken. We include the Tristachersee because it is definitely charming and the atmosphere remains 'small' despite the 42 bedrooms. We would happily spend our holiday watching the colours of the lake change a hundred times a day, from brilliant blue in sunshine to soft green in the rain. Every room in the hotel faces either the water or the woods, with not a car in sight.

Josef 'Pepi' Kreuzer began his successful hotel career here 30 years ago and he jumped at the chance of returning to take over the property. That was a decade ago. After a complete face-lift, his meticulous standards have been met. Bedrooms are expensively-furnished, paintings are chosen with care and even the indoor swimming-pool has a mural. All public rooms are large, light and airy, especially the conservatory right on the water. Even the obligatory, wood-panelled *Stube*, named for Emperor Maximilian, who hunted here, is spacious. The award-winning restaurant reflects Pepi's passion for food, especially local fish such as trout, zander and pike. This is a sophisticated retreat where luxury is tempered by informality.

Nearby skating, swimming in lake, skiing, hiking.

9900 Lienz, Tristachersee
Tel (04852) 67666
Fax (04582) 67699
Location on secluded lake; ample car parking
Meals breakfast, lunch, dinner, snacks
Prices rooms SS-SSSS with breakfast; reductions for children
Rooms 32 double, 10 single; all have bath or shower, central heating, phone, TV, radio, hairdrier, safe
Facilities 4 dining-rooms, 2 sitting-rooms, bar; terrace, large indoor swimming-pool, woods, lake, fishing
Credit Cards not accepted
Children very welcome
Disabled suitable access; lift/elevator **Pets** accepted
Closed mid-Oct to mid-Dec; restaurant, never **Languages** English, French, Italian
Proprietors Kreuzer family

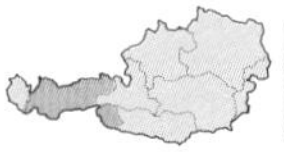

Tirol

❄ **Apartment hotel, Mayrhofen** ❄

Landhaus Veronika

Readers' comments confirm that Martin and Vroni Huber were right to choose quality rather than quantity when they built their hotel with just nine apartments back in 1984. Only 5 minutes' walk from the middle of this popular resort village, yet surrounded by fields, the Veronika is "somewhere between a castle and a farmhouse", according to son Bernhard: you have the luxury of the first combined with the cosiness of the second. Family treasures abound: old pictures on the walls, carved figures in niches, and hand-painted targets on the landings.

On one floor, green is the theme colour; on another it is red, but every apartment is different and all reflect Frau Huber's taste. "The advantage we have is that when the weather is poor, guests can use their rooms without feeling cramped." The *Kellerbar* is used for breakfast as well as snacks but no other meals are served. Mayrhofen has plenty of good restaurants, so the Hubers decided not to compete; they do serve breakfast, however, but it is ordered individually rather than taken from a buffet. Some prefer to have breakfast in their apartments, with fresh rolls delivered to their doors.

Nearby Penkenbahn cable car; winter sports; tennis.

6290 Mayrhofen 250b
Tel (05285) 3347
Fax (05285) 3819
Location on edge of village; ample car parking
Meals breakfast, snacks
Prices rooms SS-SSSS for 2, without breakfast
Rooms 9 apartments, all have bath and shower, central heating, phone, TV, minibar, *Kachelofen*
Facilities dining-room, bar; terrace, garden, sauna, whirlpool, solarium
Credit Cards not accepted
Children welcome
Disabled not suitable
Pets accepted
Closed Nov
Languages English, some French
Proprietors Huber family

Tirol

❄ **Modern chalet hotel, near Reutte** ❄

Hotel Fürstenhof

Although this hotel expanded dramatically in 1994, reports from Germany, France and Belgium insist that it deserves to stay in the book. Parents of teenagers in particular have praised the extensive sports facilities.

The emphasis on activities is not surprising since the original owners were ski stars Harti Weirather and Hanni Wenzel. Since the Kuppelhuber family bought the place, they have added an indoor swimming-pool and doubled the number of bedrooms. Although these are modern and practical, they are rather box-like.

The sitting-rooms, however, are designed for socializing, with squashy leather sofas and padded bench seats. Youngsters have their own games room and there is a mirror-walled aerobics room plus a sauna and steam bath in the basement. With its big terrace, broad lawns and tennis courts, the Fürstenhof has the feel of an American country club. Snacks even include a club sandwich and there is spaghetti on the children's menu. Otherwise, the à la carte menu is international, with French onion soup and scampi, as well as Austrian *Schnitzel* and *Käsespätzle*. The Hahnenkamm ski lift is only 5 minutes' walk away

Nearby ski-lift, cross-country trails, tennis, hiking.

6600 Wängle/Holz, Reutte
Tel (05672) 4234
Fax (05672) 423420
Location on hillside in hamlet of Wängle, near Reutte; ample car parking
Meals breakfast, lunch, dinner, snacks
Prices DB&B from SS-SSSS
Rooms 38 double; all with bath or shower, central heating, phone, TV
Facilities 3 dining-rooms, sitting-room, bar, TV room, conference room; terrace, fitness facilities, indoor swimming-pool, tennis court
Credit Cards AE, DC, MC, V
Children very welcome
Disabled not suitable
Pets accepted; not in restaurant **Closed** never
Languages English, Italian, French, Spanish
Proprietors Kuppelhuber family

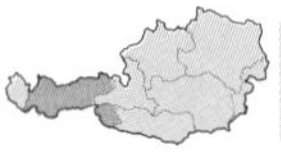

Tirol

❄ Mountain hotel, Schwaz ❄

Hotel Grafenast

'It's the steepest chairlift I have ever been on,' one reader reported. Equally nerve-jangling is the 10 km (6 mile) drive up from the valley to the hotel, but everyone agrees that it is well worth it for the views at 1330 m. It was back in 1907 that the grandfather of the present owners built a hut for toboggan enthusiasts. This is now the Grafenast's popular *Stube*. With its dark-brown wood and green *Kachelofen,* this is the heart what has grown into a comfortable health and beauty resort.

The Unterlechners, however, are true Tyroleans, so all the fun and games guests expect when staying half way up an Austrian mountain are also included, from musical evenings to walks in the woods with flaming torches. Although the chef has awards for his health-conscious cooking, hearty eaters are as happy as slimmers. The bedrooms are pretty and snug, with floral pink carpets and plenty of plain wood, but few guests spend much time in them, especially in winter. The ski school is one minute away, while the chair lift conveniently stops outside the door on its way to the Kellerjoch ski area (2030 m). Best of all, the hotel's lone television set is almost impossible to find.

Nearby fishing, golf, hiking, tennis; winter sports.

6130 Schwaz, Am Hochpillberg
Tel (05242) 63209
Fax (05242) 6320999
Location on the Hochpillberg mountain; ample car parking
Meals breakfast, lunch, dinner, snacks
Prices SS-SSS with breakfast
Rooms 17 double, 11 single; all have bath or shower, telephone
Facilities 2 dining-rooms, 3 sitting rooms, sauna, solarium, fitness and health centre; garden, swimming-pool
Credit Cards DC
Children very welcome
Disabled not suitable
Pets accepted
Closed Nov to mid-Dec; after Easter to early June
Languages English, French, Italian, Greek
Proprietors Hansjörg and Marianne Unterlechner

Tirol

❄ **Modern hotel, Seefeld** ❄

Hotel Viktoria

What do you do if your parents already run a popular hotel in Seefeld like the Veronika? Paul Kirchmair and his wife, Andrea, decided to open somewhere completely different. Where else is there a hotel with themed bedroom suites based on Madison Avenue, La Dolce Vita and Prinz Eugen? Let alone an English butler, Hungarian pictures and Italian chairs? The rotunda-like sitting-room is open-plan. Floor-to-ceiling windows look over the town, glistening wood floors reflect jade-green silk chairs in one corner, big red-black-and-green armchairs stand in another, and there is a chic bar at the back.

The suites, however, are difficult to assess. The background for each is the same: cream walls, big windows, and bold curtains. Our inspectors liked the dramatic 5 Tibetans suite with its Chinese screen, black lacquer furniture and bold red flower fabric. They hated the Montmartre's chocolate-box pictures of Parisian scenes and were stunned by La Dolce Vita, with its Spanish avant-garde furniture and bold Miró-like colours. Quality abounds but whether you like one of Austria's smallest 5 star hotels or not depends on personal taste.

Nearby winter sports; golf, tennis, hiking.

6100 Seefeld, Geigenbühelweg 589
Tel (05212) 4441
Fax (05212) 4443
Location on edge of town; car parking in underground garage
Meals breakfast, lunch, dinner, snacks
Prices DB&B SSSS for 2; children up to 16 free in parents' room
Rooms 14 suites; all have bath and shower, central heating, phone, TV, radio, minibar, hairdrier
Facilities dining-room, sitting-room, bar, billiard room, health spa, terrace
Credit Cards AE, DC, MC, V
Children welcome
Disabled easy access; lift/elevator **Pets** accepted **Closed** 4 weeks after Easter **Languages** English, French, Italian
Proprietors Kirchmair family

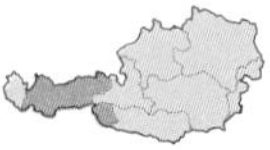

Tirol

❄ Mansion hotel, Seefeld ❄

Wildsee Schlössl

We have received mixed reviews for this unusual small hotel on the outskirts of Seefeld. However, the favourable reports outweigh the criticism. Anna Enn-Schwarz, who took over the place in 1992, now has a partner and promises to restore the standards of service demanded by our readers, who expect to meet the owner as well as the staff during a stay.

Most guests take half-board, and are rarely disappointed by Manfred Zaglacher's cooking. 'It is good Austrian cooking; a little bit nouvelle, but basically authentic Viennese cuisine.' So *carpaccio* might be followed by vegetable soup and salad from the buffet. Choose between loin of veal or venison with wild mushrooms and potato strudel and follow that with plums in an almond sauce.

The bedrooms here come in different shapes and sizes, up steps, round corners and down corridors. Room 302 has the circular tower, where guests like to watch the sun set. Room 202 opens on to the garden and is particularly popular with the ever-increasing number of golfers who enjoy both the special rates and the short walk to the course, which borders the hotel. Readers confirm that rooms at the back are the quietest.

Nearby golf, tennis, swimming; winter sports.

6100 Seefeld, Innsbruckerstr 195
Tel (05212) 2390
Fax (05212) 239012
Location on approach to Seefeld, by Wildsee; public car parking across street
Meals breakfast, lunch, dinner
Prices DB&B SS-SSS; reductions for children
Rooms 18 double, 2 single; all have bath or shower, central heating, phone, TV, radio
Facilities 3 dining-rooms, sitting-room, bar, terrace; garden, sauna, steam bath
Credit Cards AE, DC, MC, V
Children very welcome
Disabled not suitable
Pets accepted
Closed Nov; April: check with hotel
Languages English, French, Italian
Proprietors Schwarz family

Tirol

❄ Village inn, Strassen ❄

Strasserwirt

East Tirol is a backwater by Austrian standards: quiet, with few tourists and even fewer hotels. "It's a bit behind the times," admits Elisabeth Bürgler, whose family has run the inn in the heart of Strassen since 1862. What was the village meeting point for over 350 years was transformed a decade ago when a new wing was added. Instead of a few tourists dropping in for lunch, those in the know came to take advantage of the unspoiled hikes and climbs in the Dolomites in summer, as well as the cross-country skiing from the door, and the downhill at the Hochprutzertal, 4 km away.

The builders used old wood to lend atmosphere to the extra 24 bedrooms, which are traditional rather than folksy. Four rooms have four-poster beds, while downstairs, guests have their own sitting area, reading and television rooms. Chef Werner Gander has a fine reputation for his traditional Tirolean dishes as well as more health-conscious organic products.

The Strasserwirt has long been on the route of wandering minstrels, which explains the hotel's subtitle of *Kulturgasthof*. Even today, classical and folk musicians and poets stop by to provide evening entertainment.

Nearby hiking, climbing; winter sports.

9920 Strassen
Tel (04846) 63540
Fax (04846) 635455
Location in heart of village; ample car parking
Meals breakfast, lunch, dinner
Prices rooms S-SS with breakfast; reductions for children
Rooms 30 double; all have bath or shower, central heating, phone, TV, radio, hairdrier
Facilities 2 dining-rooms, 2 sitting-rooms, bar, TV room, terrace; garden; health spa
Credit Cards MC, V
Children very welcome
Disabled not suitable
Pets accepted
Closed Nov to mid-Dec; 2 weeks after Easter
Languages English, French, Italian
Proprietor Elisabeth Bürgler

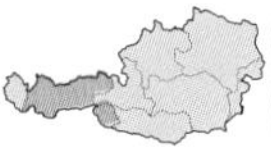

Tirol

Restaurant with rooms, Zirl

Hotel Goldener Löwe

Zirl is a small town, just off the motorway west of Innsbruck. The Goldener Löwe is arguably its main attraction. Businessmen flock here to eat; children are enchanted by the pony-sized, stuffed brown bear in the entrance hall and delight in riding on its back. The Plattner family have owned the inn for generations, but when Otto Plattner took over the Europa Hotel in Innsbruck, he left his daughter and son-in-law, Andreas Liepert, in charge. Standards have been maintained.

When our inspectors arrived some diners were tucking into a delicate terrine of trout or spinach fritters, followed by a mixed grill of both freshwater and sea fish or the traditional *Tafelspitz*. Desserts were tempting: a white chocolate mousse with mocha sauce and poppy-seed pancakes with rum cream.

Nearly half the bedrooms are singles, emphasizing the number of guests who are on business. Padded leather doors are studded; inside, trouser presses stand waiting. Slowly the rooms are being refurbished. The *Appartments* are particularly impressive with plenty of sitting space, complete with large armchairs. The bathrooms have grey-veined marble and whirlpool baths.

Nearby Fragenstein castle; Telfs; Innsbruck.

6170 Zirl
Tel (05238) 2330
Fax (05238) 263138
Location in middle of town; car parking at rear
Meals breakfast, lunch, dinner, snacks
Prices rooms SS-SSS with breakfast
Rooms 9 double, 11 single, 8 suites; all have bath or shower, central heating, phone, TV, minibar; some air-conditioning, hairdrier
Facilities 3 dining-rooms, bar; sauna
Credit Cards AE, DC, MC, V
Children welcome
Disabled access via lift/elevator at rear
Pets accepted
Closed 6 Jan to 1 Feb
Languages English
Proprietors Plattner-Liepert family

Tirol

❄ Resort hotel, Berwang ❄

Edelweiss

By building on a semi-circular dining room, the Sprengers have made their Tyrolean-style hotel bright and welcoming. Sauna, whirlpool. Three ski-lifts are within walking distance. Slopes ideal for beginners and low-intermediates.

■ 6622 Berwang **Tel** (05674) 84230 **Fax** ((05674) 842329 **Meals** breakfast, lunch, dinner, snacks **Prices** rooms S-SSS with breakfast **Rooms** 19, all with bath or shower, central heating, phone, radio **Credit Cards** not accepted **Closed** Oct to mid-Dec; after Easter to early June **Languages** English

❄ Old inn, Ebbs ❄

Hotel Unterwirt

The Steindl's hotel is in the middle of Ebbs, a small Tyrolean village known for its summer concerts and Haflinger horses. The Unterwirt, with its decorated windows, is best known for its light, regional dishes served in an authentic Stube.

■ 6341 Ebbs **Tel** (05373) 2288 **Fax** (05373) 2253 **Meals** breakfast, lunch, dinner, snacks **Prices** rooms S-SS with breakfast **Rooms** 25, all with bath or shower, central heating, phone, TV, radio **Credit Cards** AE **Closed** Nov to mid-Dec; 1 week after Easter **Languages** English, French; some Spanish

❄ Resort hotel, Fügen ❄

Hotel Haidachhof

This standard, chalet-style, modern hotel is surprisingly luxurious inside with an indoor swimming-pool and à la carte restaurant. Gretl Heim's warm welcome and the nearby Spieljoch lift ensure a regular flow of both families and couples.

■ 6263 Fügen, Hochfügenestr 280 **Tel** (05288) 2380 **Fax** (05288) 338866 **Meals** breakfast, lunch, dinner **Prices** rooms SS-SSS with breakfast **Rooms** 26, all with bath, shower, central heating, phone, TV **Credit Cards** AE, DC, MC, V **Closed** Nov to mid-Dec; 1 week after Easter **Languages** English, some Italian

❄ Town hotel, Fulpmes ❄

Hotel-Garni Hubertus

Regular skiers from as far afield as the USA and Holland are repeat visitors in this informal, turn-of-the-century bed-and-breakfast that overlooks the bandstand. Sound value, with indoor swimming-pool and sauna. Skiing on Stubai Glacier.

■ 6166 Fulpmes, Medrazerstr 20 **Tel** (05225) 62294 **Fax** (05225) 62741 **Meals** breakfast **Prices** rooms S-SS with breakfast **Rooms** 27, all with shower, central heating, radio **Credit Cards** not accepted **Closed** never **Languages** some English

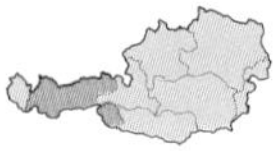

Tirol

❄ Chalet hotel, Fulpmes ❄

Hotel Atzinger

Located in Medraz, on the edge of Fulpmes. Facilities are right up-to-date, including a solarium and children's playroom. The Atzinger family make a point of using local products - eggs, milk, butter and cheese. Value for family holidays.

■ 6166 Fulpmes, Sonnegg 22 **Tel** (05225) 63135 **Fax** (05225) 6313534 **Meals** breakfast, lunch, dinner, snacks **Prices** rooms S-SSS with breakfast **Rooms** 30, all with bath or shower, central heating, phone, TV **Credit Cards** not accepted **Closed** Nov to mid-Dec; 4 weeks after Easter **Languages** English

❄ Country inn, Gnadenwald ❄

Alpenhotel Speckbacher

Good food and informality attract both holidaymakers and locals from Innsbruck to this expanded inn. Children swim in the pond, parents relax in the garden. Dark country furniture, simple rooms. Useful base for walking and cross-country skiing.

■ 6060 Gnadenwald, St Martin **Tel** (05223) 52511 **Fax** (05223) 5251155 **Meals** breakfast, lunch, dinner, snacks **Prices** rooms S-SSS with breakfast **Rooms** 21, all with bath or shower, central heating, phone; most with TV **Credit Cards** AE, DC, MC, V **Closed** Nov; 2 weeks after Easter **Languages** English, French, Italian

❄ Country guest-house, Hinterriss ❄

Herzoglicher Alpenhof

In one of Tyrol's prettiest valleys, this rustic hotel needs no frills to attract guests to the Karwendel conservation area. Open fires, red-and-white-checked duvets and farmhouse food keep hikers happy in summer, cross-country skiers in winter.

■ 6200 Hinterriss **Tel** (05245) 207 **Fax** (05245) 20711 **Meals** breakfast, lunch, dinner, snacks **Prices** rooms S-SS with breakfast **Rooms** 20, all with bath or shower, central heating, phone **Credit Cards** not accepted **Closed** Nov to mid-Dec; April to mid-May **Languages** English, Italian

❄ Resort hotel, Igls ❄

Hotel Ägidihof

Ernst Skardarasy's comfortable and traditional inn has plain wood panelling, rustic furniture in the Tiroler Stube, deep armchairs in the sitting areas and an international menu. Five minutes from ski-lifts, Kurpark, tennis, and golf driving range.

■ 6080 Igls, Lanserstr **Tel** (0512) 377108 **Fax** (0512) 377485 **Meals** breakfast, lunch, dinner, snacks **Prices** rooms SS-SSSS with breakfast **Rooms** 26, all with bath or shower, central heating, phone; TV on request **Credit Cards** AE, DC, MC, V **Closed** never **Languages** English, French, Italian

Tirol

❄ Historic inn, Innsbruck ❄

Romantikhotel Schwarzer Adler

Reports are still mixed about this 400-year old institution in the heart of the old city. The restaurant, with its low arches, pulls in locals and tourists for regional dishes and impressive wines. When staying overnight, ask for a newly-decorated bedroom.

■ 6020 Innsbruck, Kaiserjägerstr **Tel** (0512) 587109 **Fax** (0512) 561697 **Meals** breakfast, lunch, dinner, snacks **Prices** rooms SS-SSS with breakfast **Rooms** 26, with bath or shower, central heating, phone, TV, radio, minibar, hairdrier **Credit Cards** AE, DC, MC, V **Closed** never; restaurant only, Sun **Languages** English, French, Italian

❄ Resort hotel, Kitzbühel ❄

Hotel Resch

Don't be put off by the busy Wienerwald café at street-level. The Resch has comfy seats in the sitting areas and a pretty, pale blue restaurant. Quieter rooms are at the back. The bonus is nearness both to the Hahnenkamm cable car (4 min) and the Aquarena.

■ 6370 Kitzbühel, Petzoldweg **Tel** (05356) 2294 **Fax** (05356) 5006 **Meals** breakfast **Prices** rooms S-SSS with breakfast **Rooms** 22, all with bath or shower, central heating, phone, TV **Credit Cards** AE, DC, MC, V **Closed** mid-Oct to 1 Dec; mid-April to mid-May **Languages** English, French, Italian

❄ New hotel, Kufstein ❄

Lanthalerhof

Built in the traditional style, this modern hotel is lavish with marble as well as heavily-carved, pale wood panelling. Bedrooms are white, with soft greys and reds; the garden is peaceful. Near the Riedel glass factory. Own ski-bus to Schiwelt-Söll.

■ 6330 Kufstein, Schopperweg 28 **Tel** (05372) 64105 **Fax** (05372) 6410535 **Meals** breakfast, lunch, dinner, snacks **Prices** rooms S-SS with breakfast **Rooms** 20, all with bath or shower, central heating, phone, TV, radio **Credit Cards** not accepted **Closed** never **Languages** German only

❄ Resort hotel, Lermoos ❄

Silence-Sporthotel Zugspitze

With yellow umbrellas on the terrace and the Zugspitze Mountains in the background, the temptation is to sit and do nothing at this secluded hotel. However, Irene Scheiderbauer organizes cycling tours and torch-lit tobogganing. Near Hochmoos ski-lift.

■ 6631 Lermoos, Innsbruckerstr 51 **Tel** (05673) 2630 **Fax** (05673) 263015 **Meals** breakfast, lunch, dinner, snacks **Prices** rooms SS-SSS with breakfast **Rooms** 30, all with bath or shower, central heating, phone, TV, radio **Credit Cards** not accepted **Closed** mid-Oct to mid-Dec; 4 weeks after Easter **Languages** English, Italian

❄ Village inn, Matrei in Osttirol ❄

Hotel Panzlwirt

The Panzl family tree, painted outside, goes back to 1786, so we expected tradition, not the jade green, steel and wood bar where locals mix with guests back from skiing the Goldried slopes. Bedrooms are comfortable if unremarkable. Good for families.

■ 9971 Matrei in Osttirol, Tauerntalstr 4 **Tel** (04875) 6518 **Fax** (04875) 65188 **Meals** breakfast, lunch, dinner, snacks **Prices** rooms S-SSS **Rooms** 22, all with bath or shower, central heating, phone, TV, radio **Credit Cards** not accepted **Closed** never **Languages** English, Italian

❄ Resort hotel, Mutters ❄

Hotel Sonnhof

Marianne Ullman's modern hotel offers above-average comfort and is ideal for families with small children, thanks to a large garden, a proper indoor swimming-pool and nearby skiing. Only a 5-minute walk to the middle of the village.

■ 6162 Mutters, Burgstall 12 **Tel** (0512) 573747 **Fax** (0512) 584500 **Meals** breakfast, lunch, dinner, snacks **Prices** rooms S-SSS with breakfast **Rooms** 28, all with bath or shower, central heating, phone, TV, radio **Credit Cards** not accepted **Closed** mid-Oct to mid-Dec; after Easter to early May **Languages** English, Italian

❄ Old inn, Nassereith ❄

Hotel Schloss Fernsteinsee

Mad King Ludwig of Bavaria loved the brilliant green Fernsteinsee lake. He would also love this eccentric hotel, on a sharp bend in the road. The outrageous marble and gilt fittings extend even to the lavatories. Not to everyone's taste.

■ 6465 Nassereith **Tel** (05265) 5210 **Fax** (05265) 52174 **Meals** breakfast, lunch, dinner, snacks **Prices** rooms S-SSS with breakfast **Rooms** 20, all with bath or shower, central heating, phone, TV **Credit Cards** not accepted **Closed** Nov to March **Languages** English

❄ Village inn, Oetz ❄

Gasthof Zum Stern

Oetz is full of painted houses and the Griessers' 12thC inn is no exception. Add an unusual oriel window over the entrance, wood panelling, solid oak tables and chairs in the dining-rooms and you can forgive the plastic in the bathrooms.

■ 6433 Oetz, Kirchweg 6 **Tel** (05252) 6323 **Fax** same **Meals** breakfast, lunch, dinner **Prices** rooms S with breakfast **Rooms** 14, all with shower **Credit Cards** not accepted **Closed** never **Languages** some English

Tirol

❄ Resort hotel, St Anton am Arlberg ❄

St Antoner Hof

Fun, Tyrolean-style, with an indoor pool, jazz piano and new Austrian cooking as well as old beams, painted furniture and four-poster beds. This is where affluent young skiers come for the mixture of luxury and tradition.

■ 6580 St Anton am Arlberg **Tel** (05446) 2910 **Fax** (05446) 3551 **Meals** breakfast, lunch, dinner, snacks **Prices** rooms SS-SSS with breakfast **Rooms** 31, all with bath or shower, central heating, phone, TV, radio, safe **Credit Cards** DC, MC, V **Closed** Nov to mid-Dec; after Easter to mid-June **Languages** English, French, Italian

❄ Resort hotel, Seefeld ❄

Hotel Garni Almhof

The Reindl family took a lot of trouble over this attractive chalet, built on the edge of Seefeld in 1989. The new wood is heavily carved, fabrics are in soft, warm shades. 3 minutes from Geigenbühel ski area, tennis courts. Own cabin on nearby lake.

■ 6100 Seefeld, Geigenbühelstr 746 **Tel** (05212) 3066 **Fax** (05212) 306651 **Meals** breakfast, snacks **Prices** rooms S-SSS **Rooms** 14, all with bath or shower, central heating, phone, TV, radio; some with kitchenette **Credit Cards** V **Closed** mid-Oct to mid-Dec; early April to early June **Languages** English

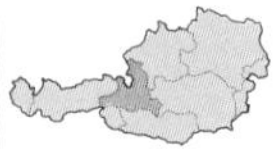

Salzburgerland

Area introduction

Salzburgerland

Salzburg and its state have both a rich landscape and a rich history. Mozart is virtually synonymous with the old city which celebrates its love of the arts during the annual Festival. All around are mountains and lakes, perfect for skiing and sailing.

Roughly triangular in shape, Salzburg province is like an iceberg: while Salzburg itself may be the most visible attraction, nine-tenths of the landscape is equally attractive.

Salzburg itself is dominated by the Hohensalzburg fortress. At its foot are magnificent buildings such as the baroque Cathedral, St Peter's abbey, the Residence of Salzburg's Prince-archbishops and, of course, Mozart's birthplace. Salzburg also boasts great chefs and restaurants, some of which have elegant bedrooms in which to sleep off a fine meal.

The southern extremity is blocked by Austria's highest mountain, the Grossglockner, as impressive a peak as there is in Europe. The Grossglockner High Alpine Road provides a giddy drive in summer. A little to the north is the smaller but significant Honigkogel, or Honeyhill, near Zell am See, which claims to be the geographic centre of Europe. Towns such as Hallein grew rich on the salt from the nearby mines.

We enjoyed the cluster of lakes to the north of the city, where hotels offer the chance of a short commute into Salzburg. Towns and villages such as Badgastein, Filzmoos, Kaprun/Zell am See, Saalbach/Hinterglemm and Goldegg show the range of ski resorts available: busy and grand, sporty and small, or just plain tiny and charming.

Much of the province's natural beauty has been preserved in national parks, especially the Hohe Tauern and the valleys of the Lungau, Pongau and Pinzgau. Again, small hotels abound.

For further details about the area, contact:
Salzburger Land - Tourismus,
Salzburg State Board of Tourism,
Alpenstrasse 96,
A-5300 Hallwang bei Salzburg
Postfach 1
Tel: (0662) 6688
Fax: (0662) 668866

This page acts as an introduction to the features of Salzburgerland. The long entries for this state – covering the hotels we are most enthusiastic about – start on the next page. But do not neglect the shorter entries starting on page 82: these are all hotels where we would happily stay. In addition to the hotels reviewed in the next 24 pages, we have also compiled a list of the charming small hotels that are within 80 km/1 hour's drive of Salzburg. See the bottom of page 187.

Salzburgerland

❄ Spa hotel, Badgastein ❄

Haus Hirt

We are pleased that our readers agree that this epitomizes the best of small Austrian hotels, run by a family who are truly professional hoteliers. Wedged high above Badgastein, the 70-year old building looks a little dour as you drive up the Kaiserpromenade. Any misgivings, however, are dispelled immediately by big vases of fresh flowers, Persian carpets on parquet floors, armchairs that look inviting and views northwest over the Gastein Valley.

Kurt Raschhofer's hobby is interior decorating and he loves English fabrics, hence the deep gold William Morris print on the *chaise-longue* in room 57. Some bedrooms are split-level, with a sitting-room downstairs and the bed and bathroom upstairs.

Throughout, the traditional blends with the modern. The Biedermeier Room has a piano, library and cupboard full of games but the broad, low-level bar with leather swivel chairs looks strictly 1990s. The breakfast buffet is particularly impressive, with 14 herbal teas, half a dozen home-made jams and bread so delicious that guests often take a loaf home.

One floor is dedicated to relieving stress, with everything from mud baths to aromatherapy and a fine indoor pool.

Nearby winter sports; walking, casino.

5640 Badgastein, Kaiserpromenade
Tel (06434) 2797
Fax (06434) 279748
Location on steep road above town; 4 garages
Meals breakfast, dinner, snacks
Prices rooms SS-SSSS with breakfast
Rooms 8 double, 4 single, 13 suites; all have bath or shower, central heating, phone, TV, radio, minibar, hairdrier, safe
Facilities dining-room, 4 sitting-rooms, bar; health farm, swimming-pool
Credit Cards AE, DC, MC, V
Children welcome
Disabled accessible via lift/elevator **Pets** accepted
Closed mid-April to mid-May; mid-Oct to mid-Dec
Languages English, French, Italian, Dutch
Proprietors Raschhofer family

Salzburgerland

❄ Converted villa, Badgastein ❄

Villa Solitude

Back in 1838, this idyllic villa was the only building overlooking the famous Gastein falls. Surprisingly, it still offers peace and quiet, despite being on the main road and next door to the casino, since all six bedrooms are at the back, looking over the valley. In 1990, the Blumschein family rescued this minor treasure and recreated the romance of the 19thC with antiques and silk fabrics.

Each room reflects a previous owner or visitor. The Kaiserin Sissy Suite has a double bed tucked into a panelled alcove; the Kaiser Wilhelm Suite retains the original large, square, wooden floor tiles but now sunshine-yellow curtains frame the tall French windows. A small breakfast room and library with fireplace complete this tiny time-machine.

Having restored the old, the Blumscheins installed the new. Rooms have fax points and satellite TV; bathrooms are regal, with the ribbon-and-tassel motif repeated on thick dressing gowns. Guests are encouraged to use the excellent Brasserie restaurant next door and the swimming and health facilities at the Grüner Baum hotel - both owned by the Blumscheins. Readers have singled out the Villa as a 'special spot' for romantic breaks.

Nearby Casino, walking, winter sports.

5640 Badgastein, Kaiser-Franz Joseph Str 16
Tel (06434) 51010
Fax (06434) 51013
Location in middle of Badgastein, overlooking falls; car parking outside, 3 garages
Meals breakfast
Prices rooms SSSS for 2 with breakfast
Rooms 5 double, 1 suite; all have bath or shower, central heating, phone, TV, minibar, hairdrier, fax point, safe
Facilities terrace, small library; sports and health facilities at Grüner Baum
Credit Cards AE, DC, MC, V
Children accepted but not suitable
Disabled not suitable
Pets not accepted
Closed May, Nov
Languages English, French, Italian
Proprietors Blumschein family

Salzburgerland

❄ **Mountain village hotel, Filzmoos** ❄

Hotel Hubertus

On our first visit, we were impressed by the quality and imagination of Johanna Maier's cooking. Since then, she has been awarded the title of Austria's 'chef of the year'. No wonder bookings must be made in advance to eat in the Art Deco-influenced purple and white formal restaurant. Despite this reputation for gourmet dining, we are pleased that Austrian traditions of hospitality continue. Throughout the day, walkers and skiers drop by for light meals as well as coffee and cake in the café or on the terrace.

This is very much a family enterprise. Dietmar Maier produces an excellent wine list and also teaches fly-fishing on the nearby lakes and rivers. Eldest son Tobias is up early to bake breakfast rolls (the hazelnut are especially good) while the youngest son was observed stealing a slice of chocolate cake on his way to school. The eight-course gourmet dinner on Thursday is excellent value, as are the winter ski-breaks which include lift passes.

'Better than ever' is our verdict on this modern, angular hotel, where the ground floor is open-plan, with big windows, while above, bed rooms are a fresh-looking combination of pale pine, white walls and green carpets with glassed-in balconies.

Nearby winter sports, walking, fishing.

5532 Filzmoos, Am Dorfplatz
Tel (06453) 204
Fax (06453) 2066
Location in middle of village; car parking in own garage
Meals breakfast, lunch, dinner, snacks
Prices rooms S-SSS with breakfast
Rooms 9 double, 2 single, 4 family, with bunk beds in separate rooms; all have bath or shower, central heating, phone, TV
Facilities 2 dining-rooms, bar, terrace, sauna, solarium, steam bath
Credit Cards not accepted
Children very welcome
Disabled lift/elevator, Room 11 suitable
Pets accepted **Closed** end-April to mid-May; mid-Oct to early Dec **Languages** English, French, Italian, some Dutch
Proprietors Maier family

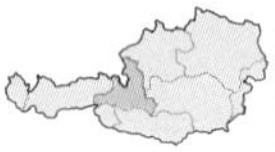

Salzburgerland

❄ Country inn, Goldegg ❄

Hotel Seehof

Goldegg is a village of preserved old houses, restored cobbled streets and no modern development. This large white inn is 500 years old. Three chestnut trees shade the entrance which leads straight into a comfortable sitting area and bar. Guests stretch out on bench seats with a novel from the bookcase or chat in the cosily-grouped armchairs. Informal enough for children to relax, it is nice enough for them to mind their manners.

Water-colours line the walls and a large battle flag hangs above the stairs which creak as you go up to the rooms. Five have blue-painted peasant furniture but all have white walls with flowery curtains and cheerful red and green cushions. "It has been an inn since 1727 and we're the fourth generation of Schellhorns to run it," says Karola who was the chef for 20 years. Now her son, Sepp, is in charge, producing gossamer-thin strudel pastry to envelope apple or rhubarb. Father Franz leads guests on cross-country or downhill ski safaris in winter and plays golf with them in summer. There is also ice-skating and curling on the frozen lake which, in warm weather, is perfect for swimming.

Nearby old village, castle, winter sports, lake, walking, 9 hole golf course.

5622 Goldegg am See
Tel (06415) 81370
Fax (06415) 8276
Location at end of village, overlooking the lake; car parking beside hotel
Meals breakfast, lunch, dinner, snacks
Prices DB&B SS-SSSS; reductions for children
Rooms 18 double, 7 single, 2 family; all have bath or shower, central heating, phone, radio, TV, safe
Facilities dining-room, 3 sitting areas, bar, games room, terrace, sauna, steam bath
Credit Cards DC, MC, V
Children very welcome
Disabled not suitable
Pets accepted
Closed April; Nov
Languages English, French, Italian
Proprietors Schellhorn family

Salzburgerland

❄ Village inn, Leogang ❄

Kirchenwirt

Another welcome addition to the new edition, the Kirchenwirt comes highly recommended by both families and skiers. The building, dating from 1326, is the oldest in the valley. Many of the medieval features are still visible: thick walls, low vaulted ceilings and carved wood. By comparison, the Unterrainer family are newcomers with only a century of ownership behind them. Sepia-coloured photographs of ancestors line the bright, white walls; the next generation are already involved.

Despite its age, this is a light, airy hotel 'where people, rather than history, come first', according to one regular. The restaurant has a fine reputation for its traditional Austrian dishes, with *Schnitzel* and *Gulasch* praised. Bedrooms are plain but comfortable but the best have impressive tiled bathrooms, with plenty of space for shaving kits and make-up bags.

In the meadows at the edge of Leogang, a new annexe, the Ansitz Wirtsgut, has striking modern apartments for longer stays. A ski lift and cross-country trails are at the door, while a free shuttle bus connects with the extensive Leogang/Saalbach/Hinterglemm ski area.

Nearby hiking; winter sports.

5771 Leogang
Tel (06583) 216
Fax (06583) 459
Location in village; ample car parking
Meals breakfast, lunch, dinner, snacks
Prices DB&B SS-SSS
Rooms 17 double, 4 apartments; all have bath or shower, central heating, phone, TV, radio, hairdrier
Facilities dining-room, sitting-room, bar
Credit Cards not accepted
Children welcome
Disabled limited acces, lift/elevator
Pets welcome
Closed Nov; after Easter to May
Languages English, French, Italian
Proprietors Unterrainer family

Salzburgerland

Converted brewery, Mattsee

Iglhauser Schloss-Bräu

The current owner of this imposing hotel is the fifth Jakob Iglhauser; his son, who is training to join the business, is Jakob VI. The Iglhausers, however, account for only a fraction of the history of the premises. Hospitality has been dispensed here since 1200, and although the hostelry and brew-house of long ago were much simpler, the bustle of activity was much the same. Waiters hurry from the kitchen past the reception desk and into the dining-rooms: one decorated with murals and a collection of pewterware; another, less formal, with bench seats and *Kachelofen.*

Frau Iglhauser is in charge of the kitchen and it is her collection of dolls that welcomes visitors in the entrance hall. Bedrooms have white walls and forest-green fabrics that set off ancient beams and floors. Bathrooms are up-to-date, however, and there are even a few four-poster beds. The Iglhausers are enthusiastic hoteliers, adding new bedrooms and hosting seminars and weddings. Guests are encouraged to use the hotel's own sailing dinghies, rowing boats and windsurfing boards. Not the place for complete relaxation, perhaps, but fun for children and with Salzburg half an hour away, handy enough for city visits.

Nearby lake, water sports; Buchberg National Park; Salzburg.

5163 Mattsee, Schlossbergweg 4
Tel (06217) 5205
Fax (06217) 520533
Location on edge of town, on lake Mattsee; car parking around hotel, garage
Meals breakfast, lunch, dinner, snacks
Prices rooms SS-SSSS with breakfast
Rooms 29 double, all have bath or shower, phone, central heating, TV, hairdrier
Facilities 3 dining-rooms, conference and banqueting facilities; terrace; free water sports
Credit Cards MC, V
Children very welcome
Disabled not suitable
Pets accepted
Closed 2 weeks end Oct
Languages English, French
Proprietors Iglhauser family

Salzburgerland

❄ **Purpose-built farm hotel, Mittersill** ❄

Nationalparkhotel Felben

We are rarely impressed by brand-new hotels but this is an exception. Surrounded on three sides by fields but close enough to walk into the village, the Scharler family's 1989-vintage hotel is next to the cleanest farmyard we have ever seen. Cows, chickens and horses delight the children of parents who, understandably, book up early to stay here.

Bedrooms are big enough for boisterous families, with attractive pink duvets, pale mauve carpets and solid wood furniture. The attention to detail deserves applause for the baby-changing facilities outside the basement lavatories and the provision of crayons and paper in the vaulted dining room. There are no compromises, however, on the food, which includes home-made jams, cheeses and even herbal teas. Half-board guests are offered a choice of meat, fish or vegetarian dishes.

The emphasis here is on health and fitness, with non-smoking bedrooms and restaurant areas and a swimming-pool heated year-round. Gunter, the fitness expert and ski instructor, leads the programme of activities for children, summer and winter.

Nearby Hohe Tauern National Park, museum, winter sports, riding, walking.

5730 Mittersill
Tel (06562) 4407
Fax (06562) 478572
Location in village of Felben, on edge of Mittersill; car parking outside hotel
Meals breakfast, lunch, dinner, snacks
Prices DB&B SS-SSS; reductions for children
Rooms 16 double, 4 single, 8 suites; all have bath or shower, central heating, phone, TV, minibar, hairdrier, safe
Facilities 3 dining-rooms, bar, games rooms; garden, health and fitness centre, heated swimming-pool, bicycles
Credit Cards not accepted
Children especially welcome
Disabled not suitable **Pets** not accepted **Closed** Nov to mid-Dec; after Easter to Ascension
Languages English
Proprietors Franz and Barbara Scharler

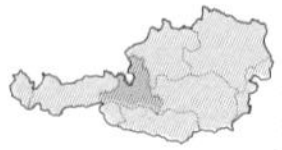

Salzburgerland

Country inn, Salzburg (at Anif)

Romantik Hotel Schlosswirt

This is where locals bring their out-of-town friends to show them a typical, old Salzburgerland inn. When the Grafs took over the guest-house of the nearby castle back in 1962 they were determined to "put the soul back in the building." They also decided to leave the austere, tunnel-like entrance hall rather than alter the architecture unnecessarily. Wooden benches in the *Gaststube* date from 1607, with antlers and a grandfather clock for decoration. The dining-rooms look turn-of-the-century with green walls, wood floors and old oil paintings.

The sense of history persists upstairs where framed pages of 19thC magazines about hunting and mountaineering hang on the walls. Each bedroom is different: number 5 has a plaid pink and red theme, number 8 has butter yellow and green fabrics, and number 17 boasts a large sleigh bed and overlooks the stream and garden at the back.

"We never wanted a fancy hotel," insists Heimo Graf. "Even our food is traditional though the quality has risen in 20 years." Across the street, the 15thC Kramerbauer annexe also has comfortable rooms with balconies.

Nearby Salzburg 20 min; cycling, golf, riding tennis, swimming.

5081 Anif bei Salzburg
Tel (06246) 72175
Fax (06246) 721758
Location on main road, on outskirts of Anif; ample car parking, garage
Meals breakfast, lunch, dinner, snacks
Prices rooms SS-SSSS with breakfast
Rooms 20 double, 7 single, 1 suite; all have bath or shower, central heating, phone, TV, fax point
Facilities 3 dining-rooms, sitting-room, conference room; garden
Credit Cards AE, DC, MC, V
Children welcome
Disabled suitable
Pets accepted
Closed Feb
Languages English, French, Italian
Managers Graf family

Salzburgerland

Country inn, Salzburg (at Elixhausen)

Romantik Hotel Gmachl

We were concerned to hear that the Gmachl family had added a new wing to their hotel. Despite this increase in size, however, visitors insist that the ambience here remains small and charming. The outside of the original inn cannot have changed much since the first Gmachls moved here back in 1583. Inside, white walls and moss-green bench seats show off the pale old wood in the reception area.

The *Kaiserzimmer*, the original tavern, is now a gourmet restaurant where diners duck through a low, carved wooden doorway. The less formal *Gaststube* has a bottle-green *Kachelofen* covered in biblical scenes. Bedrooms are in the new *Haupthaus* annexe and the *Klosterhof*, a converted barn across the street. Furnished in 'contemporary country' style, these are pretty, light and airy.

All the Gmachls are involved. Fritz's *Metzgerei* (butcher's) provides villagers as well as guests with his famous *Bratwurst*. It is no suprise that the daughters are skilled riders, since the hotel has its own riding school and stables. With six tennis courts as well as the heated swimming-pool, this is as useful for families as it is for culture-lovers visiting Salzburg.
Nearby Salzburg (20 minutes).

5161 Salzburg-Elixhausen
Tel (0662) 4802120
Fax (0662) 48021272
Location in middle of village; car parking outside hotel
Meals breakfast, lunch, dinner, snacks
Prices rooms SS-SSSS with breakfast
Rooms 41 double, 4 single, 3 suites all have bath or shower, central heating, phone, TV, radio; most have hairdrier
Facilities 3 dining-rooms, breakfast-room, bar; garden, heated swimming-pool, sauna, solarium, tennis courts, stables
Credit Cards AE, DC, MC, V
Children very welcome
Disabled several rooms adapted **Pets** accepted
Closed 1-15 July; restaurant only, Sun, Mon
Languages English, French, some Italian
Proprietors Gmachl family

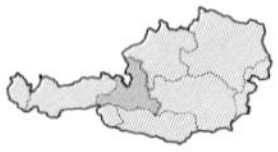

Salzburgerland

Chalet hotel, Salzburg (at Elsbethen)

Hotel Schwaitlalm

'The high point of our stay must be the friendly but very high quality service. No matter how busy they were, the owners always made time to talk to us.' A letter from a satisfied English couple confirms that it is worth the drive up from Glasenbach.

The road leads along switchbacks, through woods and finally alpine meadows, to this hotel. The Schwaitlalm, once a shingled farmhouse, is over 400 years old but the hunting lodge next door is even older. Since Lucia and Domenico Birenti took over the property in 1991, they have redecorated bedrooms, using pale colours and unusual fabrics. Again, 'quality' is the word that recurs in readers' reports.

The *Stube* has cornflower-blue table cloths and curtains with framed hand-written recipes from an old book on the walls. The dining-room is more formal but also has views south across the valley to the hills of Germany. The menu, like the Birenti family, is Austro-Italian, with *carpaccio* and ravioli, *Tafelspitz* and *Topfenknödel*. 'Delicious sweets rounded off a fine meal,' was another compliment. The hotel is popular with families, thanks to its tennis, a large indoor swimming-pool and sauna/solarium.

Nearby hiking trails; Salzburg (15 min).

5061 Elsbethen bei Salzburg
Tel (0662) 625927
Fax (0662) 6296063
Location in hills near Salzburg; ample car parking
Meals breakfast, lunch, dinner, snacks
Prices rooms SSS-SSSS with breakfast
Rooms 14 double, 3 suites; all have bath or shower, central heating, phone, TV, radio, minibar
Facilities dining-room, conference room, terrace, sauna, solarium, indoor swimming-pool, tennis court
Credit Cards MC, V
Children very welcome
Disabled access to restaurant only **Pets** accepted **Closed** early Jan to end Feb
Languages English, French, Italian
Proprietors Lucia and Domenico Birenti

Salzburgerland

Suburban villa, Salzburg

Rosenvilla Hotel Garni

The Fleischhakers are well-known as the chefs of the award-winning Pfefferschiff restaurant in Hallweg. When they opened a small bed-and-breakfast hotel early in 1996, our readers were soon in touch. They commended the 'cellar to attic' renovations, which produced a 'plain yet pretty look with an exclusive atmosphere'. The bedrooms have hand-made furniture from Mittersill and pale, restful colours.

Petra Fleischhaker is German, Klaus comes from northern Austria. Both travelled the world, cooking on cruise ships, in Scandinavia, France and Switzerland, then settled in Salzburg because of their love of music. Breakfast on the terrace in summer is idyllic, overlooking a large park with mature trees. In the evenings, guests are offered appetisers such as *carpaccio* or local cheeses, with wines from the Pfefferschiff restaurant's extensive list. "Most guests go out for dinner, but we can always provide a gourmet cold supper if they prefer to stay in." Guests who share the owners' appreciation of Salzburg's cultural attractions are catered for, since the manageress, Mrs Maier, can get tickets for concerts and exhibitions.

Nearby Salzburg.

5020 Salzburg, Höfelgasse 4
Tel (0662) 621765
Fax (0662) 6252308
Location near middle of Salzburg; ample car parking
Meals breakfast, snacks
Prices rooms SS-SSSS with breakfast
Rooms 11 double, 4 single; all have bath or shower, central heating, phone, TV, radio, hairdrier
Facilities breakfast-room; terrace, garden
Credit Cards MC, V
Children welcome
Disabled not suitable
Pets accepted
Closed never
Languages English
Proprietors Fleischhaker family

Salzburgerland

Castle hotel, Salzburg

Hotel Schloss Mönchstein

We half-expected to see Rapunzel leaning out of the 14thC tower of this imposing and well-known hotel, built on a crag above the heart of Salzburg. Instead, we found guests in shorts and open-neck shirts ordering coffee and cake on the terrace. Inside, highly-polished tables and gold plush sofas are reflected in large, gilt mirrors. It all looks very stiff and formal, yet the uniformed staff are young and friendly. Two contrasting dining-rooms offer food for the international clientele: one is named for the Empress Maria Theresa, whose portrait stares down at the green satin chairs and pale apricot linen; next door, the Paris-Lodron is all dark wood and burgundy walls.

Bedrooms are plush without being over-decorated. Number 32, high up under the eaves, is decorated in garden greens; number 11 has a tapestry on the wall. Others, too, have antiques but all have modern bathrooms. Half look over the city, the other half over the gardens and extensive park. Used by businessmen and touring North Americans and Japanese, it also has guests who settle in for a week at a time. Weddings take place in the small chapel and there are weekend harp concerts.

Nearby Casino; city of Salzburg, reached by Mönchsberg-Lift.

5020 Salzburg, Mönchsberg Park 26
Tel (0662) 8485550
Fax (0662) 848559
Location above Salzburg; car parking outside and in garage
Meals breakfast, lunch, dinner, snacks
Prices rooms SSSS with breakfast
Rooms 17 double; all have bath or shower, central heating, phone, TV, minibar, hairdrier, safe
Facilities 2 dining-rooms, sitting-rooms, bar; terraces, tennis court
Credit Cards AE, DC, MC, V
Children welcome **Disabled** access to restaurant and bedrooms with lift/elevator
Pets accepted; not in restaurant **Closed** never
Languages English, French, Italian, some Japanese
Manager Hubert Hirz

Salzburgerland

City hotel, Salzburg

Hotel Stadtkrug

Even on a chill, rainy afternoon, the Stadtkrug made a favourable impression on our inspector. The manageress greeted him, answered the telephone and welcomed a returning guest, all at the same time and without appearing flustered. That typifies the character of this hotel, which has not been overwhelmed by the year-round influx of tourists. Set in the 800-year old 'new town', it was completely renovated in 1990. Now the ancient beams are exposed above the bar, the stone arches set off white walls and a lump of granite protrudes behind reception, showing where the hotel is built into the Kapuzinerberg.

Most of the bedrooms have the same deep pink carpet, printed curtains, and no-nonsense furnishings, but room 102 boasts a four poster bed. Its bathroom looks straight out of Hollywood but even ordinary bathrooms have two wash-basins and large, well-lit mirrors. Room numbers are hand-painted, in similar style to the Papageno on the elevator doors. The restaurant is one of the most popular in town, staying open late during the Festival. In fine weather, the 4 terrace gardens offer views of church domes and spires.

Nearby Festspielhaus; Dom; Mozarteum; Mirabellgarten.

5020 Salzburg, Linzergrasse 20
Tel (0662) 873545
Fax (0662) 879588
Location in pedestrian zone in old town; parking with hotel ticket or in public car park 2 minutes away
Meals breakfast, lunch, dinner, snacks
Prices rooms SS-SSSS with breakfast
Rooms 31 double, 2 single; all have bath or shower, central heating, phone, TV, radio; some minibar
Facilities 2 dining-rooms, 3 sitting-rooms, bar, 4 terraces
Credit Cards AE, DC, MC, V
Children welcome
Disabled not suitable
Pets accepted **Closed** early Feb to mid-March; restaurant only, Tues except during Festival **Languages** English, French, Italian
Proprietors Lucian family

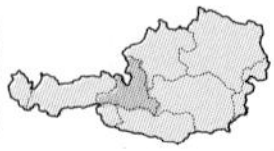

Salzburgerland

Suburban villa, Salzburg

Villa Pace

Every great city needs a special, secret hideaway. This is it. Set in the quiet residential area at the foot of the Gaisberg, the Villa Pace (formerly Haus Ingeborg) is a small luxury hotel that attracts actors, conductors, and other celebrities who relish the seclusion. The view is worthy of a tourist board poster: across meadows and trees to the castle, towers, and spires of Salzburg. The 400-year old villa has old beams and hand-woven carpets, rough walls and polished antiques.

A small kitchen with two lady chefs provides a short menu of 'new regional dishes' served in the tiny pearl-grey and pink 'La Pace' restaurant. The hotel is a reflection of the family: the carved heads in the bar and wood panels in the Salon came from a cinema and mill, both family businesses. Upstairs, every bedroom is an harmonious mixture of old and new. A four-poster bed has a wooden canopy and lacy bedspread; a well-known singer always takes the room with a grand piano.

The Oberrauch's have thought of everything: there is a small, heated swimming-pool, sauna and solarium ... even Riedel glasses in the minibars.

Nearby Gaisberg, Kapuzinerberg; Salzburg

5020 Salzburg,
Sonnleitenweg 9
Tel (0662) 6415010
Fax (0662) 6415015
Location in residential area; covered car parking
Meals breakfast, lunch, dinner, snacks
Prices rooms SSSS with breakfast
Rooms 6 double, 2 single, 8 suites; all have bath and shower, central heating, phone, TV, minibar, hairdrier, safe
Facilities dining-room, sitting-room, terrace; swimming-pool, sauna; free limousine service
Credit Cards AE, DC, MC, V
Children welcome
Disabled not suitable
Pets accepted
Closed Nov 1 to March 1
Languages English, French, Italian
Proprietors Oberrauch family

Salzburgerland

Old post inn, St Gilgen

Gasthof Zur Post

Most visitors to this popular resort on the Wolfgangsee are interested in its Mozart connection. The composer's mother was born in the village and his sister lived here. Even the main square is called Mozartplatz and honours the famous man with a fountain and statue. Our inspector is an architecture buff, so he was more interested in the centuries-old town hall and this inn. The Gasthof Zur Post was built in 1415 and is a 'protected' building. One look at the outside explains why: all along the front is a lively painted frieze depicting a medieval boar hunt.

Inside, the oak beams and dark stone floors continue the ancient ambience. Upstairs, peasant-style floral patterns decorate the doors. What is behind them varies. On the side, bedrooms have modern beds and muted colours against cream walls. Those overlooking the old market square, however, badly need updating. This is the problem facing Peter Lerperger, who became the owner in 1995. "Since this is a protected building, all alterations have to be approved, so we can only upgrade slowly." With luck, renovations will be finished by 1999. "Whatever I do will be in keeping with the age of this ancient building."

Nearby Mozart's mother's house, Zwölferhorn cable-car.

5340 St Gilgen, Mozartplatz 8
Tel (06227) 7510
Fax (06227) 698
Location in middle of village, opposite town hall; own car parking
Meals breakfast, lunch, dinner, snacks
Prices rooms S-SSS with breakfast; reductions for children
Rooms 10 double, 3 single; all have bath or shower, central heating, phone, TV; 5 double, 2 single with wash-basin only
Facilities 3 dining-rooms, bar, terrace; indoor swimming-pool, sauna
Credit Cards AE, DC, MC, V
Children welcome
Disabled not suitable
Pets accepted
Closed Nov
Languages English, French
Proprietors Lerperger family

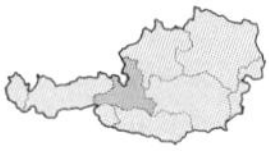

Salzburgerland

❄ Chalet hotel, Wald im Oberpinzgau ❄

Hotel Schöneben

Our inspectors did not find anywhere better than Stefan Schneider's former farmhouse at the western end of the Salzach valley. Imagine a perfect Austrian country inn, complete with sloping roof, blue shutters and wooden balconies, weighed down with geraniums. Switch to winter, with snow blanketing the mountains and scuttle inside where the rough, honey-coloured wood lines the thick walls and low ceilings, and crackling open fires bring a glow of pleasure. Stefan comes from Germany and wanted it to be "like my own house". The old china plates, rows of books, vases of dried flowers are all in the right places; the floral curtains and pink tablecloths are just the right colours. Words like 'snug', 'cozy', even '*gemütlich*' really are apt.

The same applies to the bedrooms in the older building. Despite being small, almost cramped, they are aptly-furnished in country style, with balconies. Herr Schneider cleverly expanded the hotel by building suites under the broad terrace that are 'modern rustic' in style. The only criticism we have received is from a reader who found that her bedroom (on the south side) was noisy when the windows were open.

Nearby National Park; Krimml Waterfall; winter sports; hiking.

5742 Wald im Pinzgau
Tel (06565) 82890
Fax (06565) 8419
Location above valley road, outside village; car parking outside
Meals breakfast, lunch, dinner, snacks
Prices rooms SS-SSSS with breakfast; reductions for children **Rooms** 12 double, 3 single, 9 suites; all have bath or shower, central heating, phone, TV, radio; some minibar
Facilities 3 dining-rooms, sitting-room, games-room, terrace, sauna, solarium
Credit Cards not accepted
Children very welcome
Disabled not suitable
Pets not accepted
Closed Nov to mid-Dec; after Easter to mid-May **Languages** some English, French
Proprietor Stefan Schneider

Salzburgerland

❄ **Restaurant with rooms, Werfen** ❄

Restaurant-Hotel Obauer

'Restaurant with rooms' does scant justice to this converted guest-house set among the medieval houses of Werfen. The Obauer brothers were voted 'chefs of the year' in 1989 and reservations must be made well in advance. After several years working abroad, Rudolf and Karl came home to take on the family business that stretches back 150 years. Signature dishes include a trout strudel with white wine sauce, calves' liver with truffles and chestnuts, and sumptuous desserts like blackberry and chocolate parfait, all with the light inventiveness of contemporary French chefs. The decoration is as sophisticated as the food. The two small dining rooms retain the old, low, beamed ceilings, but tables are set formally with fine linen and fresh flowers.

This contemporary feel continues upstairs where an architect friend designed dramatic, geometric headboards for the grey and white minimalist bedrooms. The white bathrooms are as antiseptic as the Obauers' kitchens. For breakfast, *brioches* and home-made breads are served to order, perhaps in the garden under gold and white umbrellas.

Nearby Schloss Hohenwerfen; the Eisriesenwelt ice caves; mountaineering; skiing; Salzburg (30 minutes away).

5450 Werfen Markt 46
Tel (06468) 75670
Fax (06468) 756712
Location on main street of village; own car parking
Meals breakfast, lunch, dinner; snacks in café
Prices rooms SS-SSS with breakfast
Rooms 6 double, 2 single; all have bath or shower, central heating, phone, TV, radio, minibar, hairdrier, safe
Facilities 2 dining-rooms; garden
Credit Cards AE
Children welcome
Disabled not suitable
Pets accepted
Closed variable, always phone ahead
Languages English, French, Norwegian
Proprietors Rudolf and Karl Obauer

Salzburgerland

❄ **Country inn, Zell am See/Thumersbach** ❄

Landhotel Erlhof

Hans Brudermann, one of Austria's top chefs, is a hard act to follow, but the Lugerbauers, who took over the Erlhof in 1994, are attracting favourable reports. This couple moved from a hotel in Mondsee, "because there are two seasons for guests here, summer and winter." They have made few changes to the old farmhouse set on the sunny, quiet side of the Zeller Lake.

Even Gustav Lugerbauer's cooking seeks to emulate that of Brudermann, with its light, modern style. Now, however, lunch as well as dinner is served in the snug dining-room with an open fire under the centuries-old, arched ceiling. Menus feature local lake fish and game from the nearby forests.

As well as eating and drinking, guests chat in the wood-panelled sitting-room, admire the view across the lake to the snow-frosted peaks of the Hohe Tauern, and sleep in plain, straightforward bedrooms. Set in spacious grounds, with lawns running down to the shore, this is a place to relax. That does not mean there is nothing to do. Some guests work off calories with golf, tennis, cycling or swimming from the Erlhof's own beach. When the lake is frozen, some diners even walk across from Zell.

Nearby Zeller Lake; mountains; winter sports.

5700 Zell am See/ Thumersbach, Erlhofweg 11
Tel (06542) 566370
Fax (06542) 5663763
Location in own grounds by lake; car parking outside hotel
Meals breakfast, lunch, dinner, snacks
Prices rooms SS-SSS with breakfast
Rooms 17 double; all have bath or shower, central heating, phone, TV
Facilities 2 dining-rooms, sitting-room, bar, terrace; sauna, solarium, fitness room, small conference facilities, garden **Credit Cards** AE, DC, MC, V **Children** accepted
Disabled not suitable
Pets accepted **Closed** Nov, 2 weeks March depending on Easter **Languages** English, French, Italian
Proprietors Andrea and Gustav Lugerbauer

Salzburgerland

❄ **Castle hotel, Zell am See** ❄

Schloss Prielau

We were impressed by this fortified manor-house on our first visit; now that Jörg Wörther has arrived, we are even more enthusiastic. Wörther, named as Austria's 'chef of the decade', sets the seal on the resurrection of Schloss Prielau. The castle, which has stood at the northern end of the Zeller lake for 600 years, was rescued from dilapidation in the mid-1980s. Paintings and carvings by local artists and craftsmen were restored, while Persian carpets were added to give warmth to tile and wood floors. The result is 'stylish informality', according to one visitor, who relished the intimacy of this hotel that takes only 24 guests.

Bedrooms are large, with curtains and chairs providing colour against white walls. Every window has a pretty view. Weekenders come from Munich, businessmen for seminars during the week, and families for skiing in winter and golf in summer. There is a private beach, while the *Prielaukirche*, a tiny chapel, is still used for services and weddings.

Anyone familiar with the relative hustle-and-bustle of Zell am See would be surprised to find such a luxurious yet secluded retreat only minutes away.

Nearby skiing in Zell, Kaprun; lake, water-sports; golf.

5700 Zell am See
Tel (06542) 2609
Fax (06542) 260955
Location north end of Zeller lake, in own park; ample car parking
Meals breakfast, lunch, dinner
Prices rooms SS-SSSS with breakfast; reductions for children
Rooms 6 double, 2 single; all have bath or shower, central heating, phone, TV, minibar
Facilities 2 dining-rooms, sitting-room with bar; terrace, sauna, private beach
Credit Cards AE, DC, MC, V
Children welcome
Disabled not suitable
Pets accepted
Closed end-Oct to early Dec; 3 weeks after Easter
Languages English, French
Managers Ursula and Jörg Wörther

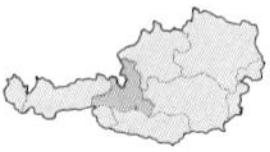

Salzburgerland

❄ Town inn, Altenmarkt ❄

Hotel-Restaurant Lebzelter

The small town of Altenmarkt is a popular base for the Zauchensee ski area. The Lebzelter, a mixture of the traditional and modern, stands in the heart of town, in a pedestrian zone. Since the hotel changed hands in 1996, readers' reports are welcome.

■ 5541 Altenmarkt 79 **Tel** (06452) 6911 **Fax** (06452) 7823 **Meals** breakfast, lunch, dinner, snacks **Prices** rooms SS-SSS with breakfast **Rooms** 29; all with bath or shower, central heating, phone, TV, minibar, hairdrier, radio **Credit Cards** AE, DC, MC, V **Closed** never **Languages** English

❄ Town hotel, Badgastein ❄

Hotel Der Lindenhof

In a sunny spot in the middle of this sophisticated resort, the Lindenhof has been in the same family for generations. The restaurant has a deserved reputation; although bedrooms are somewhat plain, they have big windows and balconies.

■ 5640 Badgastein, Poserstr 2 **Tel** (06434) 2614 **Fax** (06434) 261413 **Meals** breakfast, lunch, dinner, snacks **Prices** rooms SS-SSS with breakfast **Rooms** 22, all with bath or shower, central heating, phone, TV, radio **Credit Cards** MC, V **Closed** never **Languages** English, Italian

❄ Country hotel, Dorfgastein ❄

Unterbergerwirt

A real, red fire engine to play on, child-friendly steps and basement washing-machine, plus an excellent restaurant, keep the whole family happy. Set in meadows looking across to the Fulseck/Kreuzkogel ski slopes of the Gastein valley.

■ 5632 Dorfgastein, Unterberg 7 **Tel** (06433) 70770 **Fax** (06433) 707777 **Meals** breakfast, lunch, dinner, snacks **Prices** rooms S-SSS with breakfast **Rooms** 7, all with bath or shower, central heating, phone, TV, radio **Credit Cards** not accepted **Closed** mid-Oct to early Dec; after Easter to early May; restaurant only, Tues **Languages** English

Restaurant with rooms, Fuschl am See

Zur Sägemühle

Franz Nussbaumer decided to convert the family sawmill into a restaurant in 1976. His wife's warm welcome and good cooking make up for the roadside location. Reserve a bedroom at the back, overlooking the stream.

■ 5330 Fuschl am See 16 **Tel** (06226) 416 **Fax** (06226) 56544 **Meals** breakfast, lunch, dinner, snacks **Prices** rooms SS with breakfast (doubles only) **Rooms** 11, all with bath or shower, central heating, phone, radio; TV by request **Credit Cards** AE, DC, MC, V **Closed** Nov to late March **Languages** English, Italian

Salzburgerland

❄ Country inn, Goldegg ❄

Hotel Gasthof zur Post

Set in a pretty, unspoilt village with an old castle and church. Views are over the small lake. Winter sports plus golf, hiking, swimming, and fishing in summer. Hearty appetites appreciate the cooking, well above average, using fresh local produce.

■ 5622 Goldegg **Tel** (06415) 81030 **Fax** (06415) 810359 **Meals** breakfast, lunch, dinner, snacks **Prices** DB&B SS-SSSS **Rooms** 40, all with bath or shower, central heating, phone; TV on request **Credit Cards** V **Closed** Nov to mid-Dec; after Easter to early May **Languages** English, French, Italian

❄ Restaurant with rooms, Hallein ❄

Gasthof Hohlwegwirt

The Kronrief family are well-known for their ambitious restaurant with its imaginative sauces and regional dishes. Although renovated, this traditional Wirtshaus retains its 200 year-old atmosphere. Salzburg is only 20 minutes away; skiing at Zinkenkogel.

■ 5400 Hallein-Taxach, Salzachtal Bundesstr-Nord 62 **Tel** (06245) 824150 **Fax** (06245) 24150 **Meals** breakfast, lunch, dinner, snacks **Prices** rooms SS-SSSS with breakfast **Rooms** 5, all with bath or shower, central heating, phone, TV **Credit Cards** not accepted **Closed** never; restaurant only, Mon except during Festival **Languages** English

❄ Resort-village hotel, Kaprun ❄

Hotel Kaprunerhof

Just two minutes from the middle of Kaprun, this is a quiet hotel. The Schieferer family like to go walking, cycling and golfing with guests, who receive a discount on green fees. There are 36 holes of golf in the area.

■ 5710 Kaprun **Tel** (06547) 7234 **Fax** (06547) 8581 **Meals** breakfast, dinner, snacks **Prices** rooms S-SSS with breakfast **Rooms** 23, all with bath or shower, central heating, phone, TV, minibar, safe **Credit Cards** MC, V **Closed** never **Languages** English

❄ Holiday hotel, Leogang ❄

Hotel Rupertus

A busy, jolly small hotel with an emphasis on children and families. The Herzogs have one whole floor devoted to health and fitness, with a small lake in the grounds for summer splashing. Particularly well-priced, since a weekly barbecue and gala meals are included.

■ 5771 Leogang **Tel** (06583) 466 **Fax** (06583) 46655 **Meals** breakfast, lunch, dinner, snacks **Prices** rooms SS with breakfast **Rooms** 27, all with bath or shower, central heating, phone, TV, radio **Credit Cards** not accepted **Closed** Oct; after Easter to May **Languages** some English

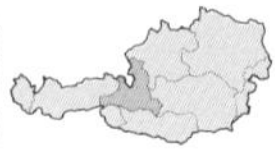

Salzburgerland

❄ Chalet hotel, Mittersill ❄

Hotel Wieser

Everyone's idea of a country hotel, with the Pinzgauer mountains beyond the meadows. Pale blue curtains and sofas brighten the reception area. Wood-panelling covers walls and ceilings. Family-oriented. Skiing at Kitzbühel-Pass Thurn, 15 minutes.

■ 5730 Mittersill **Tel** (06562) 4270 **Fax** (06562) 427056 **Meals** breakfast, lunch, dinner, snacks **Prices** rooms S-SS with breakfast **Rooms** 29, all with bath or shower, central heating, phone **Credit Cards** not accepted **Closed** Nov to mid-Dec; 1 week after Easter **Languages** English

Manor house hotel, Oberalm bei Hallein

Schloss Haunsperg

Filled with antiques and heirlooms, this 600-year old manor house is almost a museum but to the von Gernerth family it is home. Among the portraits of ancestors is great-grandfather, who wrote the words to The Blue Danube Waltz.

■ 5411 Oberalm/Hallein, Oberalm 32 **Tel** (06245) 80662 **Fax** (06245) 85680 **Meals** breakfast **Prices** rooms SSS-SSSS with breakfast **Rooms** 6, all with bath or shower, phone **Credit Cards** AE, DC, MC, V **Closed** never **Languages** English, some French, Italian

Mountain inn, Salzburg

Hotel Zistelalm

The look of a hunting-lodge or mountain hut with heavy beams and walls covered in antlers makes quite a contrast to the city down below. This hideaway, high on the Gaisberg, is especially romantic in winter, with its log fires and deep arm-chairs.

■ 5020 Salzburg, Gaisberg **Tel** (0662) 641067 **Fax** (0662) 642618 **Meals** breakfast, lunch, dinner, snacks **Prices** rooms S-SSS with breakfast **Rooms** 24, all with bath or shower, central heating, phone, TV **Credit Cards** AE, DC, MC, V **Closed** mid-Oct to mid-Dec **Languages** English

Restaurant with rooms, Strasswalchen

Zum Lebzelter

The main attraction in this town is Greti Gugg's restaurant, highly-rated for traditional dishes like stews, roasts and dumplings. Useful as an overnight stop rather than for a holiday but half-board in the plain bedrooms is good value.

■ 5204 Strasswalchen, Marktplatz 1 **Tel** (06215) 82060 **Fax** (06215) 82064 **Meals** breakfast, lunch, dinner, snacks **Prices** rooms S-SSS with breakfast **Rooms** 12, all with bath or shower, central heating, phone, TV **Credit Cards** AE, DC, MC, V **Closed** never; restaurant only, Sun evening, Mon **Languages** English

Salzburgerland

❄ Resort hotel, Wagrain ❄

Hotel Alpina

The emphasis is on sport in this comfortable, well-integrated mixture of old and new. Outsiders visit the restaurant where food is 'light traditional'. Guests can ski from the door to explore the Wagrain-Flachau slopes. Ski-school and kindergarten next door.

■ 5602 Wagrain, Kirchboden 97 **Tel** (06413) 8337 **Fax** (06413) 833750 **Meals** breakfast, lunch, dinner, snacks **Prices** rooms SS-SSS with breakfast **Rooms** 20, all with bath or shower, central heating, phone, TV, radio **Credit Cards** not accepted **Closed** Oct to early Dec; after Easter to late May **Languages** English, French, Italian

❄ Village inn, Wagrain ❄

Gasthof Grafenwirt

In the middle of this classic, flowery mountain village is the Schindlmaissers' white-painted hotel where folk ornaments brighten plain, modern rooms. Menus change daily; local lamb is a speciality. Good base for exploring Enns Valley.

■ 5602 Wagrain, Markt 14 **Tel** (06413) 8230 **Fax** (06413) 7162 **Meals** breakfast, lunch, dinner **Prices** rooms S-SS with breakfast **Rooms** 17, all with bath or shower, phone; some TV, hairdrier, safe **Credit Cards** not accepted **Closed** Tues (Apr-Oct), last 2 weeks June, Oct 20-early Dec depending on snow **Languages** English

❄ Twin hotels, Wald im Oberpinzgau ❄

Hotels Walderwirt and Märzenhof

The Strasser family combine two inns; the 15thC Walderwirt, with wood-panelled dining- rooms and intimate fireside seats, is linked by underground passage to the 20thC Märzenhof with its big, glassed-in swimming-pool and modern bedrooms.

■ 5742 Wald im Oberpinzgau **Tel** (06565) 82160 **Fax** (06565) 821614 **Meals** breakfast, lunch, dinner, snacks **Prices** rooms S-SSS with breakfast **Rooms** 20, all with bath or shower, central heating, phone, TV, radio **Credit Cards** MC, V **Closed** Nov to mid-Dec; mid-April to mid-May **Languages** English, French, Italian

❄ Chalet hotel, Zell am See ❄

Hotel 'Der Metzgerwirt'

The old building, with dark timbers punctuated by small windows and green shutters, celebrated its 500th birthday in 1993. The rooms in the annexe, built in 1990, have old wood inside and look out on to a courtyard with rose-garden. Useful for families.

■ 5700 Zell am See, Sebastian Hörl Str 11 **Tel** (06542) 72520 **Fax** (06542) 7252025 **Meals** breakfast, lunch, dinner, snacks **Prices** rooms SS-SSSS with breakfast **Rooms** 31, all with bath or shower, central heating, phone, TV **Credit Cards** DC **Closed** April, Nov **Languages** English, Italian, French

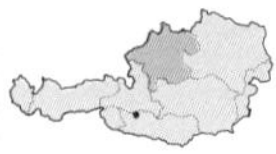

Oberösterreich

Area introduction

Upper Austria.

Upper Austria boasts a variety of landscape, including mountains like the Höllengebirge and the northern slopes of the Totes Gebirge; the broad valley of the Danube; a large part of the Salzkammergut and its lakes. Thick forest contrasts with wide, open fields.

Towns like Linz, the state capital, gave us the renowned *Linzertorte* cake while *Palatschinken*, Upper Austria's pancakes, are now regarded as a national dish. Linz mixes ancient and modern successfully. The 8th century St Martin's church and the Castle contrast with the industry of today. Thousands are attracted each year to the Bruckner Festival.

We particularly enjoyed visiting the province's small towns where laudable efforts have been made to restore and revive their centres, cleaning old buildings and pedestrianising the narrow streets. The province's cultural attractions satisfy any taste. Music-lovers regard St Florian, with Bruckner's organ and his burial place, as a pilgrimage spot, while the visual beauty of the Kaiservilla, the former imperial summer retreat, tops other visitor's lists. In the summer months, there are also vintage trains run by enthusiasts for enthusiasts who like to look back to the good old days.

Hikers and bikers head for the peace and quiet of the Mühlviertel, the Innviertel and Hausruck areas. The Salzkammergut, studded with over 70 small lakes, is particularly popular for water sports, while mountaineers practice their skills in the Phyrn-Eisenwurzen region. Everywhere our inspectors discovered the small inns and rural retreats that make a holiday so special.

For further details about the area, contact:
Landesverband für Tourismus in Oberösterreich,
Upper Austrian Tourist Board,
Schillerstrasse 50,
A-4010 Linz
Tel: (0732) 663021
Fax: (0732) 600220

This page acts as an introduction to the features of Oberösterreich. The long entries for this state - covering the hotels we are most enthusiastic about - start on the next page. But do not neglect the shorter entries starting on page 101: these are all hotels where we would happily stay.

Oberösterreich

Lakeside hotel, Attersee

Gasthof Häupl

This is still a winning combination: cooking by a top chef and views across the largest lake in the Austrian Alps. Early booking, therefore, is essential, particularly on sunny summer weekends. Even in winter, gourmets phone ahead for a table in one of the two *Stüberl*. They come for regional specialities like fish from the lake or dumplings stuffed with bacon, accompanied by one of half a dozen wines available daily by the glass, or beer from the barrel.

There has been an inn here for over 300 years. The Häupl family have run it for a mere seven generations during which they have collected some eye-catching antiques. A confessional, complete with a statue of St Florian on top, is a telephone booth; nearby is an ancient wine press. Small alcoves with tables and chairs are cosy spots for reading or chatting.

As for bedrooms, number 121 is particularly striking with its black and white *Wiener Werkstätte* (Vienna Workshop) furniture and a print of a Gustav Klimt landscape on the wall. Others are simpler, but bathrooms are slick and new, with grey or white tiles and power showers. All this, and breakfast on the terrace overlooking the Attersee.

Nearby concerts; golf, riding, water-sports, para-gliding.

4863 Seewalchen am Attersee, Hauptstr 20-22
Tel (07662) 2249
Fax (07662) 882262
Location above village on edge of lake; car parking outside
Meals breakfast, lunch, dinner, snacks
Prices rooms SS-SSSS with breakfast; reductions for children **Rooms** 34 double; all have bath or shower, central heating, phone, TV, radio, minibar; some safes
Facilities 3 dining-rooms, breakfast-room, bar, 3 conference rooms; terrace, sauna, mountain hut
Credit Cards AE, DC, MC, V
Children welcome
Disabled access to 3 rooms
Pets accepted
Closed never
Languages English, French, Italian
Proprietors Häupl family

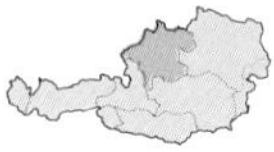

Oberösterreich

Lakeside hotel, Attersee

Gasthof Föttinger

'Do what Gustav Mahler did' is the motto of this 19thC hotel which capitalizes on the 'Mahler connection'. Inside, the large, open-plan lobby is a display case of Mahler memorabilia including some songs, a small bust of the great man and a copy of his 3rd Symphony. He wrote this, along with the 2nd Symphony, in a small summer cabin he put up by the lake. That was back in 1893-96 and he was visited by his friend, the conductor Bruno Walter, who arrived by steamer. These boats still ferry people around the lake and the garden is still used for concerts and musical evenings. The flowery meadows which were there in the composer's day are now covered by caravans.

That is the drawback to staying here. The hotel is right on the lake but views from the green-shuttered windows are blotted by a caravan park at its busiest in July and August. Otherwise, the bedrooms are all generously-sized, with white walls and modern pine furniture: 'functional' to some, 'anonymous' to others. The restaurant is similarly expansive, with a rustic look thanks to antlers and the brown colour-scheme. Meat is a speciality, since the butcher's shop has been part of the hotel since 1907.

Nearby Salzkammergut; Höllengebirge; Neukirchen Game Park.

4853 Steinbach am Attersee, Seefeld 14
Tel (07663) 342
Fax (07663) 34242
Location on edge of lake; own car parking
Meals breakfast, lunch, dinner, snacks
Prices rooms S-SS with breakfast; reductions for children
Rooms 21 double, 5 single, 2 suites; all have bath or shower, central heating, phone, TV, radio, hairdrier, safe
Facilities 3 dining-rooms, bar, lift/elevator; terrace, garden, private beach, indoor swimming-pool
Credit Cards MC
Children very welcome
Disabled restaurant only
Pets tolerated
Closed Jan
Languages English, French
Proprietors Föttinger family

Oberösterreich

Lakeside villa, Attersee

Villa Langer

With porches and balconies, gables and bay windows, this is a classic 'summer resort' villa from the turn of the century. Except for the vine that now covers one wall, it cannot have changed much over the years. Our inspector was happy to settle himself on a Biedermeier sofa and read the newspaper, then take a late coffee in the sunny white conservatory.

The villa is at the south-east corner of the Attersee. Behind, a rocky, wooded cliff veers up steeply; in front is the water. Unfortunately, between house and shore is the road that circumnavigates the lake. Guests must cross it to reach the private boathouse with garden and windsurfers for hire.

Dinner may be booked five nights a week for those not wanting to cook. Each of the 13 suites has a kitchenette and some have two bathrooms, making them suitable for large families. Furnishings are a mixture of 19thC and modern; some rooms have original neo-Gothic painted ceilings; most have views of the lake. None have televisions. This is an informal, peaceful place in the Salzkammergut 'for those who can amuse themselves and don't need attractions'. Pets are welcome, 'but no snakes or lions'.

Nearby lake, resorts; Weissbacher Sattl; Weissenbach gorge.

4854 Weissenbach, Attersee
Tel (07663) 242
Fax (07663) 24236
Location on lake-side road at foot of Höllen mountains; own car parking area
Meals breakfast
Prices rooms SS-SSSS with breakfast
Rooms 4 double, 2 single, 13 apartments with kitchenettes; all have bath or shower, central heating, phone, radio, minibar, hairdrier
Facilities 2 dining-rooms, breakfast-room, sitting-room, bar; terrace; sauna, fitness room, table tennis room
Credit Cards not accepted
Children very welcome
Disabled not suitable
Pets accepted
Closed early Dec to early March **Languages** English, French, Italian
Proprietors Langer family

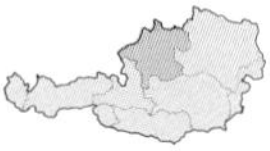

Oberösterreich

Castle hotel, Bad Hall

Schloss Feyregg

This is a 'dream *Schloss*', as full of atmosphere as it is of history. Mentioned in an 11thC chronicle, it actually goes back even further to the 8thC. The castle seen today, however, dates from 1720. The seclusion is total; as for silence, 'a cemetery would be noisier', according to our inspector. He delighted in the gardens: from the long avenue lined with statues, to the inner courtyard and wilder garden beyond. The mixture of furnishings from different ages is a happy one.

The high ceilings have a medieval look, while elaborate baroque doors lead to the breakfast-room, where paintings of 19thC society ladies adorn the walls. Each of the bedrooms has its own little sitting-room with, perhaps, a 19thC *chaise longue*, a writing desk, or prints of the Hapsburg military on the walls. This is the furniture that was in the castle when Frau Harmer's family bought it in 1937, so it still looks and feels like a private house. Josie the dachshund welcomes visitors and other small dogs.

Views are over the gardens or of the church in the sleepy little town of Bad Hall. Just below the castle is an old inn where guests often have lunch or dinner.

Nearby fishing, golf; mineral springs.

4540 Bad Hall
Tel (07258) 2591
Location just outside Bad Hall; own car parking
Meals breakfast
Prices rooms SS-SSSS with breakfast
Rooms 4 double, 2 single in castle, 3 single, 2 suites in garden annexe; all have bath or shower, central heating
Facilities breakfast-room, billiard room
Credit Cards not accepted
Children accepted if well behaved
Disabled not suitable
Pets small dogs accepted
Closed Christmas
Languages some English, French
Proprietor Ruth Maria Harmer

Oberösterreich

Town hotel, Freistadt

Gasthof Zum Goldenen Hirschen

Freistadt has managed to conserve much of its medieval heritage. The ancient moat is green with grass but the doorways, balconies and windows tell a story that is hundreds of years old. The town even has a night-watchman. This guest-house is just inside the solid Bohemian Gate and the garden backs onto the old walls. Built after the great fires of the early 1500s, it was rebuilt and given a new façade some 100 years ago.

Our inspector was delighted by the swallows in the arched passage where old wine presses and a hay cutter lend an aura of rusticity. In the vaulted, Gothic dining hall, the marriage of owners Johann and Anna Kronberger in 1867 is recorded on the ceiling, but it has been in the present family only since 1913.

The cooking is imaginative, with traditional dishes matched by, for example, a pumpernickel soufflé with cheese sauce. Bedrooms are large and some have a separate sitting area; the best offer a view across the town towards the Gothic church.

Our inspector liked the two pretty *Stüberln*, the terrace at the back, and the cheerful young owners who have expanded into the house next door.

Nearby old town of Freistadt; Mühlviertel.

4240 Freistadt, Böhmergasse 8-10
Tel (07942) 722580
Fax (07942) 721110
Location on old city street, near Böhmer Tor; public car parking
Meals breakfast, lunch, dinner, snacks
Prices rooms S-SS with breakfast; reductions for children
Rooms 26 double, 7 single; all have bath or shower, central heating, phone, TV, radio
Facilities 4 dining-rooms, sitting-room, bar, TV room, sauna, conservatory; terrace
Credit Cards DC
Children welcome
Disabled not suitable
Pets accepted
Closed 3 weeks Jan
Languages English, French
Proprietors Deim family

Oberösterreich

Castle hotel, Gmunden

Schlosshotel 'Freisitz Roith'

Most towns would be happy to have one castle; Gmunden has several. The most famous is the 17thC '*Seeschloss*'; Freisitz Roith is older by some 100 years. A coat of arms engraved above the entrance boasts of a history dating back to the 16thC. Set in a park of some seven hectares (about 18 acres), it sits grandly on a hill on the eastern shore of Traunsee lake.

The entrance is impressive: decorative wrought-iron gates open to the reception area where Renaissance chairs in carved oak look ready for a duke, if not a king. Do not expect the luxury of some castle hotels. Most bedrooms look over the water but they vary in size and style, and are priced accordingly; more if they have baroque-style beds, a good deal less for those with rather boring modern furniture. A hotel since 1968, it is popular with locals for weddings. The Prechtl family have now left but we hope that the company who are the new owners maintain, and even improve, standards. This is the sort of place people either love or hate: take the full-sized, stuffed peacock with outspread tail above the stairway. A novelty or just bizarre? If it is the latter, this is probably not the place for you.

Nearby Gmunden town hall; Schloss Ort; Grünberg cable-car.

4810 Gmunden am Traunsee, Traunsteinstr 87
Tel (07612) 4905
Fax (07612) 490517
Location on hill overlooking Traunsee; car parking in front of hotel
Meals breakfast, lunch, dinner, snacks
Prices rooms S-SSS with breakfast; reductions for children **Rooms** 20 double, 7 single, 1 suite; all have bath or shower, central heating, phone, TV, radio, minibar, safe
Facilities 5 dining-rooms, bar; terrace; gymnasium, sauna, solarium
Credit Cards AE, DC, MC, V
Children welcome
Disabled access, lift/elevator
Pets accepted
Closed never **Languages** English, French, Italian
Proprietors Firma Asamer

Oberösterreich

❄ **Mountain inn, Grünau im Almtal** ❄

Romantik Hotel Almtalhof

'This is more of an experience than a hotel. Stand on the balcony on a spring evening and breathe in the fresh, alpine air of the Alm valley. Lilac bloom in the garden below; further on is the rushing river, between birch, chestnut and sycamore trees.' Our inspector continued to enthuse about the 'wonderfully rambling, seemingly endless *Stüberl* and connecting corridors.' Around one corner is a family of straw dolls; everywhere are cushions embroidered in red and white folk designs by Ulrike Leithner, who with her husband, Karl, runs the hotel.

They are gradually improving the 1911 building, built by a Leithner grandfather. Bedrooms, for instance, are being enlarged. Karl made most of their pine furniture, including the carved four-poster bed in Number 11. Bathrooms show similar care and are fitted with power showers and gilded taps. The food is Austrian with a light touch, using produce from local farms and plenty of game. Our inspector was pleased also by the detailed wine list which includes bottles from Austria's finest vineyards. Add an indoor swimming-pool, a garden for children, and a new golf course nearby and you have 'paradise'.

Nearby golf, hiking, cycling; winter sports; Almsee.

4645 Grünau im Almtal
Tel (07616) 82040
Fax (07616) 820466
Location valley of River Alm; ample car parking
Meals breakfast, lunch, dinner, snacks
Prices rooms SS-SSS with breakfast; reductions for children
Rooms 16 double, 3 single, 2 suites; all have bath or shower, central heating, phone, TV, hairdrier, radio, safe
Facilities 2 dining-rooms, café, bar; terrace; indoor swimming-pool
Credit Cards AE, MC, V
Children very welcome
Disabled 1 bedroom specially adapted
Pets accepted
Closed mid-Oct to mid-Dec; after Easter to end April
Languages English, French
Proprietors Leithner family

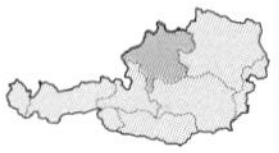

Oberösterreich

Town hotel, Kremsmünster

Hotel Schlair

A reader from Munich insists that we include his discovery, and we are delighted to agree with his enthusiastic report. Eric Kux, an American with a huge chuckle, is also an impressive chef, who trained in France and Italy. In the dining-room, which is restricted to house guests only, he serves 'Austrian dishes with a twist'. There is no set menu, since dishes are prepared from the best produce available each day in the market.

The hotel consists of two buildings. The Hotel Schlair, big and square, is in the newer part of Kremsmünster. Two minutes' walk away, up the hill near the former market place, is the quiet, 800-year old Zur alte Mühle annexe. Breakfast is worth the walk: 'I can't name the many different kinds of bread that are served ... the sweet smell of coffee and sugar early in the morning is just fantastic.' Since the breads come from the bakery next door, run by Erik's brother-in-law, this really is a family business. Although bedrooms are stylish, with the conveniences demanded by both tourists and business visitors, it is the Kux family's 'individual attention' that our reader remembers. A solo traveller, he 'never had the feeling of being ignored.'

Nearby Kremsmünster monastery.

4550 Kremsmünster, Franz-Hönig Str 16
Tel (07583) 5258
Fax (07583) 52582
Location in town; own car parking
Meals breakfast, dinner
Prices rooms SS-SSS with breakfast
Rooms 18 double, 8 single; 4 apartments with kitchens; all have bath or shower, central heating, phone, TV, radio, minibar
Facilities dining-room, sitting-room
Credit Cards AE, MC, V
Children not suitable
Disabled not suitable
Pets welcome
Closed Christmas to 8 Jan
Languages English, French, Italian
Proprietors Maria and Erik Kux

Oberösterreich

Bed-and-breakfast hotel, Linz

Wolfinger

Although this hotel is larger than our norm, readers confirm that the Dangl family maintain the standards expected in this book. There are no undiscovered gems in Linz, where the old quarter attracts tourists from all over the world. Located right on the Hauptplatz, the 19thC façade of the Wolfinger hides a history dating back hundreds of years, most recently as an inn, before that as a monastery. There is little of the monks' austerity nowadays about the comfortable rooms and tasteful furnishings. Old mirrors, photographs and Biedermeier and art nouveau furniture continue the sense of the old, but bathrooms have the very latest in fittings. Large, white-tiled and with huge mirrors, they have the strong lighting professional make-up artists like but the rest of us find cruel. Most of the bedrooms overlook the quiet, inner courtyard; a few have a view over the square.

The comings and goings on the Hauptplatz can also be seen from the breakfast room, 'if you are lucky enough to get a seat at the window.' Another feature here is the *Bürgertisch*, a table dating from 1889 and inscribed with the names of prominent city councillors. Cars may be unloaded at the door.

Nearby Pillar of the Holy Trinity, Minorite Church, Mozart Haus.

4020 Linz, Hauptplatz 19
Tel (0732) 7732910
Fax (0732) 77329155
Location on main square in pedestrian area of old town; underground public car park
Meals breakfast
Prices rooms SS-SSS with breakfast
Rooms 40 double, 4 single; 3 suites; all have bath or shower, central heating, phone, TV, hairdrier
Facilities breakfast-room, sitting-room, TV room; terrace
Credit Cards AE, DC, MC, V
Children welcome
Disabled not suitable
Pets accepted
Closed never
Languages English, French, Italian
Proprietors Dangl family

Oberösterreich

Restaurant with rooms, Mondsee

Landhaus Eschlböck

Reservations are essential if you want to sample some of the best cooking in Austria. Karl Eschlböck is the chef and his 'new Austrian' style works wonders with char and zander. Other dishes range from sole on a bed of asparagus to pot roast of duck with potato soufflé and red cabbage.

Unfortunately, the full effect of the lake-view is lessened by the main road which runs between the hotel and water. Although traffic has to slow down because of a steep bend, it remains a distraction, particularly for the bedrooms above. For this reason, these are less expensive than the quieter ones at the back. At least a tunnel under the road provides easy access to the private dock and beach. The inn dates back 400 years but this family have been here only since 1952. Karl Eschlböck has been in charge since 1972, and now his reputation attracts businessmen and weekenders as well as Salzburg Festival-goers. Our inspector found the atmosphere rather impersonal, perhaps because the emphasis is on food rather than the hotel. He did notice, however, a lectern with carved eagle which belonged to Herr Eschlböck's great-grandfather, who was Mayor of Vienna.

Nearby Mondsee parish church; Rauchhaus open-air museum.

5310 Mondsee/Plomberg
Tel (06232) 3166
Fax (06232) 316620
Location on lakeside road overlooking lake; ample car parking
Meals breakfast, lunch, dinner
Prices rooms SS-SSSS; reductions for children
Rooms 9 double, 2 single, 1 suite; all have bath or shower, central heating, phone, TV, minibar
Facilities 4 dining-rooms, bar; terrace, sauna, beach on lake
Credit Cards AE, DC, MC, V
Children welcome
Disabled ramp to upper floor
Pets accepted
Closed Jan
Languages English, French, Italian
Proprietor Karl Eschlböck

Oberösterreich

Hotel-restaurant, Mondsee

Leitnerbräu

Ever since the 1994 expansion and redecoration, we have received plaudits from readers who have been impressed by what is now a luxury hotel. It still scores for location: right in the old part of this attractive town, among pink, blue and yellow houses and opposite the church of St. Michael with its glorious baroque façade. The lake is only a 10-minute walk away. In fine weather, people like to sit outside under the red and white-striped awning; where better to people-watch?

The wrought-iron sign above, with lions rampant, hop leaves and barrel reflects the brewhouse origins of the 18thC building. The host is Olaf Marschallinger, a man who enjoys meeting people, speaks his mind and is ready to put the world to rights. His wife's domain is the kitchen, where she makes traditional Austrian specialities such as *Bauernschmaus*, a mixed meat dish with dumplings. This is not the place for dainty appetites: portions are fulsome and tasty.

The occasional Biedermeier chest of drawers, oil painting and stained glass window were retained but the overall look is cool and sophisticated, the atmosphere is genteel.

Nearby Mondsee lake; monastery; local museum.

5310 Mondsee,
Steinerbachstr 6
Tel (06232) 6500
Fax (06232) 650022
Location in middle of village; car parking in garage
Meals breakfast, lunch, dinner, snacks
Prices rooms SS-SSSS with breakfast
Rooms 30 double, 1 family; all have bath or shower, central heating, phone, radio, TV, hairdrier; some fax points
Facilities 3 dining-room, breakfast-room, bar, 2 conference rooms; sauna, fitness area; bicycle hire
Credit Cards AE, DC, MC, V
Children welcome
Disabled 2 adapted rooms; lift/elevator **Pets** accepted
Closed Nov **Languages** English, French, Italian
Proprietors Marschallinger family

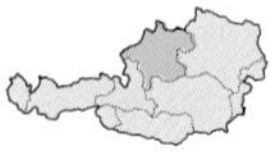

Oberösterreich

❄ **Waterside hotel, Neufelden** ❄

Mühltalhof

The Rachingers are continuing an inn-keeping tradition going back six generations. The atmosphere in their 17thC hotel is very personal: there are family photographs on the walls, and more in an album near the entrance.

Daughter Johanna runs the administrative side, mother and son do the cooking, which is much praised. Fish and game appear on the ever-changing menu which could include trout mousse with crayfish sauce and venison medallions with redcurrant jelly. Complementing the food is a well-chosen list of wines from France, Italy and Austria, including a personal supply of Styrian wines from a brother-in-law.

Not surprisingly, families enjoy the informality. The playground comes with a children's house, the old mill-pond provides swimming and rowing, and there is a private tennis-court. Over half the rooms look over the water. Those at the top of the building have small windows and wood panelling, creating an effect that could be 'small and cosy' or 'dark and cramped', according to mood and personal taste. Larger bedrooms with balconies are recommended for those with children who need to dry swimwear and towels.

Nearby Danube River; Mühlviertel; tennis, golf; winter sports.

4120 Neufelden
Tel (07282) 6258
Fax (07282) 62583
Location on a minor road, overlooking old mill-pond; ample car parking
Meals breakfast, lunch, dinner, snacks
Prices rooms S-SS with breakfast; reductions for children
Rooms 17 double, 3 single, 6 suites; all have bath or shower, central heating, phone, TV, minibar, hairdrier, safe
Facilities 3 dining-rooms, sitting-room, bar, TV room; terrace; sauna
Credit Cards AE, DC
Children welcome
Disabled not suitable
Pets accepted
Closed Nov
Languages English, French
Proprietors Rachinger-Eckl family

Oberösterreich

Lakeside hotel, St Wolfgang

Landhaus zu Appesbach

Popular demand has elevated this elegant country house to the status of a full page entry. Our readers have been swift to point out that, despite the popularity of St Wolfgang itself, a large leafy park and private access to the lake ensure total privacy and peace. Now well over a century old, the cream and green villa has neatly-trimmed lawns stretching down to the clear, clean waters of the Wolfgangsee.

Back in 1937, the Duke of Windsor, complete with houndstooth suit, stayed here following his abdication of the British throne. Much of what he enjoyed is still visible today.

The Windsor Suite, with its handsome twin beds sharing one ornate headboard, has the same glorious views over the lake; the reading-room still looks as if a dropped pin would cause consternation, while the bar, with its high stools, would be a fine set for a Noel Coward play.

The Kozma-Eidlhuber family, however, are not stuck in a time warp. Although they have preserved the heritage, they have added the best of today with saunas, a tennis court and a landing stage for sailing and windsurfing.

Nearby golf, hiking, mountain biking; water sports.

5360 St Wolfgang
Tel (06138) 2209
Fax (06138) 220914
Location in parkland; ample car parking
Meals breakfast, lunch, dinner, snacks
Prices rooms SS-SSS; reductions for children
Rooms 28 double; all have bath or shower, central heating, phone, TV
Facilities dining-room, reading-room, bar; terrace; health and fitness area; garden, dock, tennis court
Credit Cards AE, DC, MC, V
Children welcome
Disabled not suitable
Pets accepted
Closed Nov to Easter
Languages English
Proprietors Kozma-Eidlhuber family

Oberösterreich

Town inn, Schärding

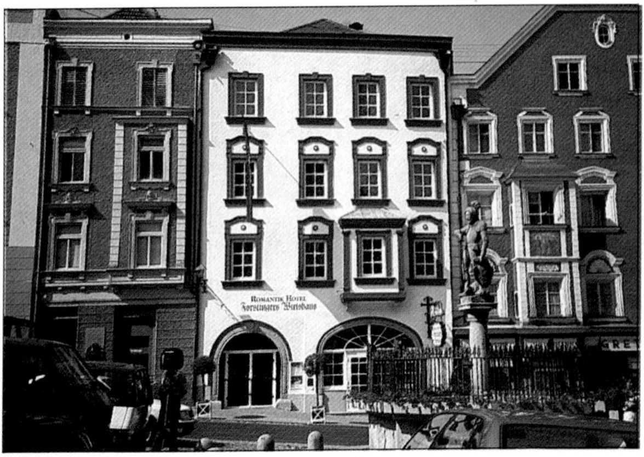

Förstingers Wirtshaus

Those readers who have stopped in Schärding have confirmed that the locals are right: their main square could well be the 'prettiest in Austria'. The look is pure story-book, with baroque houses painted ochre, red or light blue. They followed our inspector's advice to 'turn off the main street, under medieval arches to the bank of the fast-flowing Inn where swans breast the stream, mallard croak and teal fall out of the darkness and into the water like stones.'

The tavern dates back to 1606 and its interior continues the rustic traditions of days-gone-by, with old beams, vaulted ceilings and intricate carving. In the dining-room, formality rules, with pink linens, long-stemmed glasses and candle-light giving a glow to the elaborate pine panelling. The cooking is impressive, with the emphasis on fish, such as carp, *seibling*, and trout from nearby mountain streams. No doubt fly-fishermen flushed with success can have their catch cooked for dinner.

Take care when choosing a bedroom. The older, atmospheric ones, furnished with antiques, overlook the square where the Saturday market sets up at 6 am. The newer rooms at the back are quieter but have less character. Bathrooms are modern.

Nearby city of Schärding; Danube River; Passau.

4780 Schärding am Inn, Unterer Stadtplatz 3
Tel (07712) 23020
Fax (07712) 23023
Location on main square; own unattended car parking area
Meals breakfast, lunch, dinner, snacks
Prices rooms SS-SSS; reductions for children
Rooms 14 double, 2 single; all have bath or shower, central heating, phone, TV, minibar, hairdrier, safe
Facilities 2 dining-rooms
Credit Cards AE, DC, MC, V
Children welcome
Disabled not suitable
Pets accepted
Closed never
Languages English
Proprietors Förstinger family

Oberösterreich

Lakeside hotel, Attersee

Hotel-Seegasthof Oberndorfer

Right on the Attersee lake, this resort-hotel is well-known for its restaurant which specializes in lake fish. A few pieces of old furniture, but the modern bedrooms have white walls, sparse decoration and quilted bedspreads in pastel shades.

■ 4864 Attersee, Hauptstr 18 **Tel** (07666) 78640 **Fax** (07666) 786491 **Meals** breakfast, lunch, dinner, snacks **Prices** rooms SS-SSSS with breakfast **Rooms** 26, all with bath or shower, central heating, phone, radio, TV, minibar, fax point **Credit Cards** not accepted **Closed** Jan, Feb **Languages** English, French, Spanish

❄ Country hotel, Attersee at Unterach ❄

Hotel Georgshof

Set in fields above the southern end of the Attersee, the hotel's terraces maximize views of the surrounding woods and fields. Walks and tennis-courts nearby. The dining-room and bedrooms are square and box-like. Indoor swimming pool.

■ 4866 Unterach 320 **Tel** (07665) 8501 **Fax** (07665) 85018 **Meals** breakfast, lunch, dinner, snacks **Prices** rooms S-SSS with breakfast **Rooms** 25, all with bath or shower, central heating, phone, TV **Credit Cards** AE, DC, MC, V **Closed** never **Languages** English

Restaurant with rooms, Bad Hall

Hofwirt Gasthof Schröck

Four centuries of hospitality continue, with Johanna Unterreiter-Schröck's cooking drawing guests to Hehenberg on the edge of Bad Hall. Dishes include local fish such as char and carp. Comfortable rooms above. Popular with fly fishermen.

■ 4540 Bad Hall, Hehenberg **Tel and Fax** (07258) 2274 **Meals** breakfast, lunch, dinner **Prices** rooms S-SS with breakfast **Rooms** 3, all with bath **Credit Cards** not accepted **Closed** Nov; New Year; restaurant only, Mon, Tues **Languages** English, French

❄ Country guest-house, Bad Leonfelden ❄

Berggasthof Waldschenke am Sternstein

Up a forest road on the edge of the Bohemian woods and near the Czech border, this Alpine house has fresh, pretty bedrooms with floral-patterned curtains. Surprisingly smart dining-room with well-prepared food. The owner's fox-terrier rather aggressive.

■ 4190 Bad Leonfelden **Tel** (07213) 6279 **Fax** (07213) 62797 **Meals** breakfast, lunch, dinner, snacks **Prices** rooms S-SS with breakfast **Rooms** 12, all with bath or shower, central heating **Credit Cards** not accepted **Closed** Nov, Dec **Languages** English, French, Czech

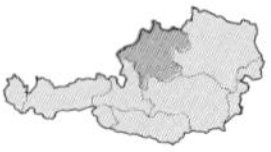

Oberösterreich

Restaurant with rooms, Bad Schallerbach

Hotel-restaurant Grünes Türl

With its sunny terrace, this 200-year old tavern is popular with locals and visitors. Doris and Ingrid Ameshofer's cooking is highly-praised, especially regional dishes of trout and venison. Newer bedrooms have bathrooms; the older ones have showers.

■ 4701 Bad Schallerbach, Gebersdorf 1 **Tel** (07249) 48163 **Fax** (07249) 42932 **Meals** breakfast, lunch, dinner, snacks **Prices** rooms S-SSS with breakfast **Rooms** 30, all with bath or shower, central heating, phone, TV **Credit cards** AE, DC, MC, V **Closed** never **Languages** English, French

Town hotel, Enns

Hotel-Restaurant Lauriacum

In contrast to the attractive 16thC houses and churches nearby, the Lauriacum has modern bedrooms, a country-style Stüberl and a secluded garden. Josef Angerer's cooking is outstanding. Used both by businessmen and holiday-makers; golf 4 km away.

■ 4470 Enns, Wienerstr 5-7 **Tel** (07223) 2315 **Fax** (07223) 233229 **Meals** breakfast, lunch, dinner **Prices** rooms SS with breakfast **Rooms** 30, all with bath or shower, TV, phone, minibar **Credit Cards** MC, V **Closed** Christmas, New Year; restaurant only, Sat **Languages** English, French, some Italian, Greek

Old inn, Freistadt

Hotel Goldener Adler

An old inn in an equally old city; part of the medieval walls are built into the hotel. Unusual glassed-in corridors overlook the covered central courtyard. Modern bedrooms are actually more pleasant than the older ones. Sauna and swimming-pool, garden.

■ 4240 Freistadt, Salzgasse 1 **Tel** (07942) 72112 **Fax** (07942) 7211244 **Meals** breakfast, lunch, dinner, snacks **Prices** rooms S-SS with breakfast **Rooms** 37, all with bath or shower, central heating, phone, TV **Credit Cards** AE, DC, MC, V **Closed** never **Languages** English, Italian, Spanish

Lakeside hotel, Gmunden

Waldhotel Marienbrücke

In a peaceful, wooded park, the Obermayr family hotel and restaurant is delightful. Fish, from the lake or sea, are a speciality, cooked with flair. Bedrooms are plain, but have been upgraded and modernized. Fly-fishing courses available.

■ 4810 Gmunden, An der Marienbrücke 5 **Tel** (07612) 4011 **Fax** (07612) 267954 **Meals** breakfast, lunch, dinner, snacks **Prices** rooms S-SSS with breakfast **Rooms** 15, all with bath or shower, central heating, phone, TV **Credit Cards** AE, V **Closed** occasionally in off-season **Languages** English, Italian

Oberösterreich

❄ Country hotel, Hinterstoder ❄

Pension Dietlgut

In an unspoilt valley, surrounded by meadows and pine forest, the Wendl family offer bedrooms and self-catering apartments. Fly-fishing and hiking in summer; cross-country trails at the door; 10 minutes' walk to Bärenalm lift for downhill skiing.

■ 4573 Hinterstoder, Hinterstoder 99 **Tel** (07564) 52480 **Fax** (07564) 524839 **Meals** breakfast, dinner **Prices** rooms SS with breakfast **Rooms** 18, all with bath or shower, central heating, phone, radio TV **Credit Cards** AE, DC, MC V **Closed** mid-Oct to mid-Dec; 2 weeks April **Languages** English, French, Italian

Cliff-top hotel, Hofkirchen

Hotel Falkner

The spectacular setting makes the Falkner family hotel special. Both open and glassed-in terraces have giddy views of the Danube. Contemporary bedrooms, traditional restaurant and sitting-rooms. Indoor swimming-pool, sauna and fitness area.

■ 4142 Hofkirchen, Marsbach 2 **Tel** (07285) 223 **Fax** (07285) 22320 **Meals** breakfast, lunch, dinner, snacks **Prices** rooms S-SS with breakfast **Rooms** 14, all with bath or shower, central heating, phone, radio **Credit Cards** not accepted **Closed** Nov to mid-Dec; mid-Jan to March **Languages** English

City hotel, Linz

Hotel Drei Mohren

The original building may date from 1595, composer Anton Bruckner may have slept here, but this is really a contemporary central, city hotel with smart, modern bathrooms. The beige and brown suits businessmen who stay here during the week.

■ 4020 Linz, Promenade 17 **Tel** ((0732) 772626 **Fax** (0732) 7726266 **Meals** breakfast **Prices** rooms S-SS with breakfast **Rooms** 25, all with bath or shower, central heating, phone, TV, minibar **Credit Cards** AE, DC, MC, V **Closed** never **Languages** English, French, Italian

Restaurants with rooms, Linz

Gasthof Goldener Adler

Near the middle of Linz, this pleasant bed-and-breakfast is a converted private house. With its modernized bedrooms and cheerful breakfast-room, this is an ideal base to explore the old city. The Nudeloper restaurant below is popular with locals.

■ 4040 Linz-Urfahr, Hauptstr 56 **Tel** (0732) 731147 **Fax** (0732) 7311475 **Meals** breakfast **Prices** rooms S-SS with breakfast **Rooms** 26, all with bath or shower, central heating, phone, TV **Credit Cards** AE, MC, V **Closed** never **Languages** English, French, Italian

Oberösterreich

Lakeside hotel, Mondsee

Seehotel Lackner

Even locals enjoy the 15-minute stroll from town to the lakeside terrace to eat Topfenstrudel while admiring the view of water and mountains. As well as water-sports, golf and tennis are available nearby. Rooms are plain but comfortable.

■ 5310 Mondsee, Gaisberg 33 **Tel** (06232) 2359 **Fax** (06232) 235950
Meals breakfast, lunch, dinner, snacks **Prices** rooms S-SSS with breakfast **Rooms** 17, all with bath or shower, central heating, phone
Credit Cards not accepted **Closed** late Nov to early Dec
Languages English

Riverside hotel, Ottensheim

Donauhof

Although the Donauhof is a square, modern block on the banks of the Danube, it is a sophisticated combination of hotel, restaurant and café. Every Thursday, the Landls have a gourmet evening. Rooms are stark, but quiet. 12 km from Linz.

■ 4100 Ottensheim, An der Fähre **Tel** (07234) 3818 **Fax** (07234) 3825
Meals breakfast, lunch, dinner, snacks **Prices** rooms S-SS with breakfast
Rooms 10, all with bath or shower, central heating, phone, TV
Credit Cards AE, DC, MC, V **Closed** never **Languages** English

Niederösterreich

Area introduction

Lower Austria

Of the nine Federal States, Lower Austria is easily the biggest, even engulfing the newest, separate state of Vienna, its former capital. St Pölten is taking on the role of the administrative headquarters.

The River Danube splits the state in two, flowing from west to east. On the north bank is the Wachau, famous for the high quality of its wines, grown on steep hillsides between Melk and Krems. Further north near the Czech border is the Waldviertel, the wooded quarter, which provides unspoilt country for walking, with plenty of wildlife and birdlife. Here the hotels and inns are harder to find, but worth searching out to experience a different sort of Austria, off the beaten track.

The range of activities on offer is impressive. Visitors can choose to follow the great cultural trails from castle to castle or even abbey to abbey, stopping at Melk and Göttweig, Klosterneuburg and Heiligenkreuz. By contrast, they can pamper themselves at any of the dozen or more health spas, bathing in thermal sulphur springs or taking peat cures. Baden has the added attraction of a glamorous casino. Requiring rather a more active lifestyle are the well-marked trails for hikes and horseback rides, as well as the ever-present skiing, which, on the Hochkar, continues well in to spring.

We spent time in the taverns in the Wachau and Gumpoldskirchen; ancient and atmospheric, these are the perfect places to try the local wines which rarely get exported, as the locals prefer to keep them for their own consumption.

A crescent of countryside to the west of Vienna itself is the famous *Wienerwald*, Vienna Woods, romanticized in waltz tunes and novels and still the area for the Viennese to enjoy a happy day out with a meal.

Some towns are part of legend, such as Dürnstein, where the minstrel Blondel found King Richard the Lionheart. We found small hotels, unblemished by the flood of tourists, where genuine hospitality is still a matter of personal pride.

For further details about the area, contact:
Niederösterreich Information,
Lower Austrian Tourist Board,
Heidenschuss 2,
A-1010 Vienna
Tel: (01) 5333114
Fax: (01) 5350319

This page acts as an introduction to the features and hotels of Lower Austria and gives brief recommendations of good hotels that for one reason or another have not made a full entry. The long entries for this state - covering the hotels we are most enthusiastic about - start on the next page. But do not neglect the shorter entries starting on page 121: these are all hotels where we would happily stay.

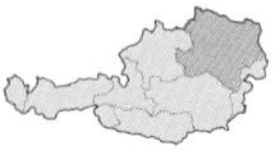

Niederösterreich

Town hotel, Dürnstein

Gartenhotel Pfeffel

'Nice, jolly owner; nice, jolly place' ends our inspector's report on this inn, where oleanders, geraniums and a walnut tree add colour to the entrance. Situated just outside Dürnstein on the riverside road, our reporter warns would-be guests to take care since it is easy to miss the abrupt turning to the hotel under a railway arch. Although the building is modern, the general look is pleasantly old-fashioned.

Where so many hotel dining-rooms in Austria are panelled in wood, this one has mirrors, making the small room look larger and providing a multi-reflection of the chandelier. The breakfast room is contemporary, with tiled floors, rush-seated chairs, and an open fireplace.

Views change with every flight of steps: the sitting area and terrace look out on the hills; some of the bedrooms face the Danube. All are spacious, with lace mats on the dark wood furniture. Like other hoteliers in this region, the Pfeffels have their own wine production, 'von den steilen Bergterassen des Schreiberberges' ('from the steep hanging terraces of the Schreiberberg' above them) and special dishes range from fish and lamb to nettle-cream soup.
Nearby Dürnstein; Danube; Wachau.

3601 Dürnstein
Tel (02711) 206
Fax (02711) 20688
Location along riverside from Dürnstein, abrupt turn under railway arch; ample car parking
Meals breakfast, lunch, dinner
Prices rooms S-SSS with breakfast reductions for children
Rooms 33 double, 5 single; all have bath or shower, central heating, phone, TV, radio, minibar, hairdrier
Facilities 2 dining-rooms, 3 sitting-rooms, bar, TV room, table-tennis room; terrace, sauna, small outdoor swimming-pool
Credit Cards MC, V
Children welcome
Disabled not suitable **Pets** accepted **Closed** Nov to March
Languages English, French
Proprietors Pfeffel family

Niederösterreich

Town hotel, Dürnstein

Gasthof Sänger Blondel

Everyone knows the legend of the minstrel, Blondel, who discovered the whereabouts of the imprisoned King Richard I of England by singing the monarch's favourite song beneath the castle battlements. Did it really happen? Who cares? The old walled town of Dürnstein and its ruined castle are still worth a visit, particularly when you stay in this yellow-painted villa.

The Schendls take care over their food, not only following regional recipes, but using plenty of organic produce. Our inspector happily devoured home-made bread and apricot jam, plum dumplings and praline chocolates. The wine list, with its detailed descriptions, makes interesting reading and even better drinking. The family have been in Dürnstein for 300 years and have been innkeepers since 1900. In this much-visited town it would be all too easy to rest on their laurels; fortunately they do not.

Colours throughout tone with the caramel-coloured oak panelling, and the terrace garden is full of flowers. Looming above is the heavily-decorated blue tower of the *Stiftskirche*. Once a week there is an evening of zither music and there are bicycles for guests to use.

Nearby Dürnstein; Danube River; Wachau.

3601 Dürnstein
Tel (02711) 253
Fax (02711) 2537
Location in Dürnstein, not overlooking river; car parking outside, 7 garage spaces
Meals breakfast, lunch, dinner, snacks
Prices rooms SS-SSSS with breakfast; reductions for children
Rooms 15 double, 1 single; all have bath or shower, central heating, phone, radio, TV, hairdrier
Facilities 3 dining-rooms; garden
Credit Cards not accepted
Children accepted
Disabled not suitable
Pets accepted
Closed mid-Nov to mid-March
Languages English, French
Proprietors Schendl family

Converted granary, Geras

Alter Schüttkasten Geras

Of the readers who have enjoyed staying here, many booked in for one of the well-known pottery and painting courses. Others came for the walking in the unspoiled woods of the Waldviertel. The hotel, a former granary, is on the outskirts of the rather ordinary village of Geras. The massive structure dates from the 17thC when it was built to store grain for the nearby monastery, which still owns the property. Walls are over one metre thick, roofs are steep, windows are small and the only decoration on the outside is a baroque stone Madonna. Luckily, the conversion to restaurant and hotel was sensitive; any temptation to over-furnish the rooms with plush curtains and fancy ornaments was resisted. The style remains simple, the atmosphere tranquil.

Hic habitat fortuna ('Here happiness reigns') reads the inscription in the lobby, where stark, white walls contrast with terracotta floor tiles. Bedrooms, with rush-seated chairs, crisp linens and a cross on the wall have a pleasingly puritanical look. The vaulted cellars, which once held the monks' wine, now have dining-tables and chairs. Menus here offer game and fish from the monastery's estates.

Nearby woods, hiking.

2093 Geras, Vorstadt 11
Tel (02912) 332
Fax (02912) 33233
Location on edge of town; ample car parking
Meals breakfast, lunch, dinner, snacks
Prices rooms SS with breakfast
Rooms 21 double, 5 single; all have bath or shower, central heating, phone, radio, minibar
Facilities 2 dining-rooms, bar, TV room; terrace; sauna, billiard-room, conservatory
Credit Cards DC
Children accepted
Disabled reasonable access; lift/elevator
Pets accepted
Closed Dec, Jan
Languages English
Proprietor Monastery

Niederösterreich

Castle inn, Haitzendorf

Schlosstaverne Grafenegg

The Hüttl family, who charmed so many of our readers, have moved on. Now the dynamic chef Toni Mörwald is in charge. He has other catering interests, so we hope that the hotel side of the business retains the charm that attracted us here in the first place.

The impressive 19thC Gothic-style Grafenegg Castle belongs to Duke Metternich-Sandor, and this castle inn has a flair and elegance reminiscent of a French château. The castle itself is well-known for its classical music concerts, which take place in the enormous indoor riding-school and feature soloists such as Alfred Brendel, who played in 1992.

Despite the grandeur of the complex, the hotel has an aura of intimacy, with comfortable bedrooms decorated in Laura Ashley style. Toni Mörwald has added minibars and safes, as well as a variety of expensive dining experiences, particularly in the summer months: a Friday night barbecue, a Saturday evening dinner in the garden and jazz lunches on Sunday. His attention to detail extends to making his own chocolates and he is happy to prepare elegant, but again luxurious picnic hampers for guests who want to explore the surrounding woods.

Nearby Krems; Danube-River; Wachau; vineyards.

3485 Haitzendorf, Grafenegg 12
Tel (02735) 2616
Fax (02735) 26166
Location in countryside, near village of Haitzendorf; ample car parking
Meals breakfast, lunch, dinner, snacks
Prices rooms SS with breakfast, reduction for children
Rooms 9 double; all have bath or shower, central heating, phone, radio, minibar, safe; TV on request
Facilities 3 dining-rooms, bar; terrace
Credit Cards not accepted
Children accepted
Disabled not suitable; restaurant access
Pets accepted
Closed Jan, Feb
Languages English
Manager Toni Mörwald

Niederösterreich

Village inn, Hinterbrühl

Die Höldrichsmühle

We are keeping an eye on this well-known inn. First, because it has expanded, and secondly, because we have had a complaint about housekeeping standards. Bedrooms in the old building were rather cramped for the price. Now, the 1994 extension has modern rooms as well as a sauna and bar.

This is where Schubert was supposedly inspired to write one of his most famous songs, *Der Lindenbaum*. The ancient lime, or linden, tree was later destroyed by lightning but Schubert's portrait still graces the doorway. He was not the only musician to enjoy hospitality here; Beethoven also stayed. The history of the building is even older than its 200 years as an inn; farmers came to this mill to grind grain as far back as 1210.

In fine weather, meals are served on the roof-terrace. The formal dining-room, serving Viennese cuisine, is in the vaulted cellars. Only 17 km from Vienna, it is popular both at weekends and for weekday business lunches. The road in front is a main one, so ask for a room at the back to be sure of a quiet night. Those who have been riding through the Wienerwald presumably sleep well; the indoor riding-school is right on the premises.

Nearby Heiligenkreuz, Vienna Woods; golf.

2371 Hinterbrühl, Gaadnerstr 34
Tel (02236) 262740
Fax (02236) 48729
Location in Vienna Woods village, 17 km from Vienna; ample car parking
Meals breakfast, lunch, dinner, snacks
Prices rooms SS-SSS with breakfast
Rooms 40 double; all have bath or shower, central heating, phone, TV, minibar, hairdrier
Facilities 5 dining-rooms; terrace; sauna, bicycles, riding stables, tennis court
Credit Cards AE, DC, MC, V
Children welcome **Disabled** reasonable access, ground floor bedrooms **Pets** accepted if not too big **Closed** 2 weeks Feb **Languages** English, French, Italian, Hungarian
Proprietors Moser family

Niederösterreich

Country restaurant with rooms, Klein Wien

Landgasthof Schickh

A 'restaurant and hotel next to the railway station' did not sound like a promising candidate, so we were surprised by the headline on our inspector's report: 'Triple A rating'. His comments were littered with exclamation marks - for the food, the surroundings and the professional yet friendly host. The building is low, painted yellow and right next to the single-track Krems St. Pölten line, 'mercifully silent at night and with very little traffic during the day' although there is the occasional blast from a locomotive. Railway buffs insist on having bedrooms overlooking the line. Everyone, however, likes to have a drink in the 80-year old railway carriage in the garden, furnished to resemble a Viennese café.

All three dining-rooms are attractive, although different in size and decoration. Regulars, including the Viennese acting fraternity, book tables in the one which suits their mood. They also sit out in the large garden, shaded by horse chestnut trees. This is where the house specialities, lobster and crayfish, are kept alive in tanks. Other dishes getting rave reviews include: trout *en gelée*, duck breast with cheese and garlic noodles, and apricot dumplings, 'the best in Austria'.

Nearby Stift Göttweig monastery.

3511 Klein Wien, Furth-Göttweig
Tel (02736) 218
Fax (02736) 2187
Location beneath hill-top monastery of Göttweig; ample car parking
Meals breakfast, lunch, dinner, snacks
Prices rooms SS-SSS with breakfast; reductions for children
Rooms 9 double, 2 single, 1 apartment; all have bath or shower, central heating, phone, TV, radio
Facilities 4 dining-rooms, bar; railway-carriage diner
Credit Cards not accepted
Children welcome
Disabled access to restaurant only
Pets accepted **Closed** never; restaurant only, Wed, Thurs
Languages English, French
Proprietor Ferdinand Schickh

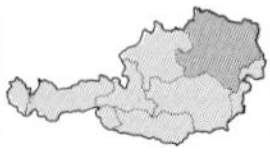

Niederösterreich

Restaurant with rooms, Krems/Donau

Am Förthof

We are happy to report that Helga Figl's programme of renovations has been completed and rooms now match the standard of her well-known restaurant. Her young team of chefs clearly know their business, serving up modern versions of traditional specialities such as *Tafelspitz* and garlic soup. Although hearty appetites might find the portions a little scant, this leaves room for the desserts, described as 'fabulous'. The inn is an oenophile's delight, with a wide range of wines by the glass and a most knowledgeable wine-waiter.

Frau Figl, who also runs a coffee and wine business in Dürnstein, took over her parents' hotel, set in a 200-year old former hunting lodge. The bedrooms are mainly white with pastel blue, pink, green or yellow. The suites are stylish also, with Biedermeier furniture.

Frau Figl encourages local artists by displaying their work and there is often a huge painting on an easel near reception. You may, or may not, like what is on show when you visit. Week-long programmes are offered, with lectures and tours on themes of churches, castles, museums and wine.

Nearby Krems and Stein old towns; wine museum; Dürnstein.

3500 Krems, Donauländе 8
Tel (02732) 83345
Fax (02732) 8334540
Location on road looking south over Danube; car parking outside
Meals breakfast, lunch, dinner, snacks
Prices rooms SS-SSS with breakfast; reductions for children
Rooms 20 double, 2 suites; all have bath or shower, central heating, phone, TV, radio
Facilities 2 dining-rooms, TV room; terrace; small outdoor swimming-pool
Credit Cards DC, MC, V
Children welcome
Disabled not suitable
Pets accepted
Closed never
Languages English, French, Italian
Proprietor Helga Figl-Kraus

Niederösterreich

❄ **Health farm, Lackenhof** ❄

Biohotel Jagdhof

You do not have to take the cure to feel healthy here; just gazing on meadows, hills and woods is therapeutic for city folk. The 20-year old building was remodelled in 1990 and is now a *Biohotel*. This means that natural fibres and materials are used in furnishings and a master switch in bedrooms can cut off all electrical current while guests sleep.

Frau Borbath is in charge of the kitchen; her motto is 'natural and light', with an emphasis on whole food menus incorporating plenty of organic fruit and vegetables. Although she is an enthusiast for the healthy way of eating, she is no dietary despot; regional specialities are also offered, plus home-made breads and herb *Schnaps*. The *Biostub'n* is a no-smoking zone, as are the Tower Suites and one entire floor of bedrooms. Fitness fans swim in the heated outdoor swimming-pool, play tennis on the clay court, practice golf shots on the driving range and hike the 150 km of marked trails. Fly-fishing, para-gliding and river-rafting can be arranged. In winter, the ski-lift on Ötscher mountain is just 150 m away. We would be happy to stay put and have massages, cosmetic treatments and spa baths.

Nearby hiking, tennis; golf; winter sports.

3295 Lackenhof am Ötscher, Weitental 95
Tel (07480) 3000
Fax (07480) 3008
Location at foot of Ötscher mountain; ample car parking **Meals** breakfast, lunch, dinner, snacks
Prices rooms SS-SSSS with breakfast; reductions for children **Rooms** 16 double, 3 single, 4 suites for 4-6 people; all have bath or shower, central heating, phone, TV, radio **Facilities** 3 dining-rooms, sitting-room, bar; terrace, gymnasium, health spa, heated outdoor swimming-pool, garden
Credit Cards AE, DC, MC, V
Children welcome **Disabled** not suitable **Pets** accepted
Closed 2 weeks Nov; 2 weeks after Easter **Languages** English, French
Proprietors Borbath family

Niederösterreich

Country retreat, Mayerling

Hotel Kronprinz Mayerling

Despite the change of hotel name, the food in the famous restaurant is as consistent as ever, according to the gourmets among our readers. The Kronprinz is one of Austria's top 50 restaurants. Its name reflects the continuing fascination for the mysterious and tragic suicide pact between Crown Prince Rudolf and the beautiful Baroness Marie Vetsera. It all happened 100 years ago at the royal hunting-lodge in nearby Mayerling. Nowadays, the hotel's high prices may promote suicidal tendencies among ordinary folk but they do not seem to deter business clients from Vienna. Thankfully, prices in the simpler Landgasthof Marienhof restaurant are affordable.

Chestnut and lime (or linden) trees surround the hotel, which was once an inn for the famous monastery in Heiligenkreuz, not far away. Travellers of old would be astounded by the spacious bedrooms, each with a whirlpool bath, let alone the creations of chef Heinz-Viktor Hanner. No detail is overlooked; herbs are grown in his own garden, the wine list runs to 200 vintages from France, Spain, Italy and Austria, and there is even a *Käse-Somelier* who selects cheeses for ripening in a special cellar.

Nearby tennis; riding; Heiligenkreuz.

2534 Mayerling 1
Tel (02258) 2378
Fax (02258) 237841
Location in country between Mayerling and Heiligenkreuz; ample car parking
Meals breakfast, lunch, dinner, snacks
Prices rooms SS-SSS with breakfast; reductions for children
Rooms 23 double, 5 single, 4 suites; all have bath or shower, central heating, phone, TV, radio, minibar
Facilities 3 dining-rooms, bar; terrace; gymnasium, health spa
Credit Cards AE
Children welcome
Disabled not suitable
Pets accepted
Closed never
Languages English, French, Italian
Proprietors Hanner family

Niederösterreich

Castle hotel, Mühldorf

Burg Oberrana

Special experiences rarely come cheaply, but this one is worth every penny. The Nemetz family rescued this romantic, Renaissance castle from dilapidation a decade ago. Standing on a hill above the Danube valley, a castellated wall protects the 900-year old building with its steep grey roofs, sheer white walls and windows high above ground level. The crypt beneath the handsome, Romanesque chapel is 200 years older; the oldest, in fact, in Austria. Oberrana is secluded, with views to every point of the compass over wooded hills, valleys and pasture. The interior has been sympathetically restored, the beamed ceilings and white arches balanced by thick Persian carpets and clusters of pictures, a traditional *Kachelofen* and a grandfather clock.

Bedrooms and suites have well-chosen antique furniture; one of the best is the single with a four-poster baroque bed, curtained in green. Bathrooms are rather small, perhaps because of the difficulty in building them into such a massive structure. We would happily while away the time watching deer grazing in the inner moat while sipping one of the manager's home-made apple or apricot brandies.

Nearby Wachauer Tal, Krems.

3622 Mühldorf bei Spitz/Donau
Tel (02713) 8221
Fax (02713) 8366
Location on crest of hill above village; ample car parking
Meals breakfast, snacks
Prices rooms SS-SSSS with breakfast; reductions for children
Rooms 7 suites, 4 double, 2 single; all have bath or shower, central heating, phone, TV, radio
Facilities breakfast-room, sitting-room, bar, TV room; terrace, garden
Credit Cards AE, V
Children very welcome
Disabled not suitable
Pets accepted
Closed 1 Nov to 1 May
Languages English
Managers Stierschneider family
Proprietors Nemetz family

Niederösterreich

Riverside inn, Raabs an der Thaya

Hotel Thaya

Any hotel on the banks of a river, overlooking an 11thC castle, has to have a head start over its rivals. Raabs itself is a sleepy little village in what many Austrians consider to be a backwater, bordering Czechoslovakia.

The squat yellow inn dates from 1890. From the main street, guests step straight into the bustling *Stüberl*, which has a slightly French brasserie air about it, perhaps because of the old lithographs in art nouveau frames. The smaller dining-room has pine-framed booths with green velvet cushions. In the larger restaurant, a mural depicts costumed villagers from 1300 to 1900.

The bedrooms are in the addition, built in 1987. Picture windows look over the garden, or even better, lead on to balconies overhanging the river itself. Decoration is simple in cool greys and whites; bathrooms are compact but practical.

This is a sports-oriented hotel, with canoeing on the still, green Thaya River. Franz Strohmer leads trips himself and also takes guests on excursions into Czech Republic. Cooking is above average, with hearty local dishes plus international favourites.

Nearby Raabs Castle, Rosenburg falconry; water-sports, tennis, riding, squash.

3820 Raabs an der Thaya
Tel (02846) 2020
Fax (02846) 20220
Location on main street of village, overlooking river; own car parking
Meals breakfast, lunch, dinner, snacks
Prices rooms S-SS with breakfast; reductions for children
Rooms 27 double, 3 apartments; all have shower, central heating, phone, TV
Facilities 3 dining-rooms, sitting-room, bar, TV room; terrace, garden; gymnasium, sauna
Credit Cards not accepted
Children very welcome
Disabled not suitable
Pets accepted with advance notice **Closed** 2 weeks Feb; restaurant only, Tues dinner
Languages English
Proprietors Strohmer family

Niederösterreich

❄ **Health farm, near Reichenau** ❄

Knappenhof

The drive from Reichenau to this hotel is a thoroughly enjoyable one through lush pastures and orchards. The Knappenhof, built in 1907, stands on the southern slopes of the Rax. Fresh flowers and a large wrought-iron chandelier dominate the entrance-hall and big wooden peasant chests stand in corridors. Bedrooms are in relaxing shades of pale blue or pink, with white walls covered in pictures of mountains. Two rooms at the back are rather gloomy; the rest have splendid views.

Kurhotels sometimes have a rather austere atmosphere, as if healthy regimes preclude enjoyment, particularly where food is concerned. Angela Puskas has other ideas and her award-winning food wins converts because it is imaginative and full of both flavour and variety. Butter, oil and cream are avoided. Instead, herbs and other natural flavourings are used to enhance fish, meat and organic vegetables. Even wild rice is prepared like an Italian risotto. The hotel also boasts a non-smoking dining-room. This is where Angela keeps her family of teddy bears, a collection that has grown since childhood. She also owns the popular restaurant Kanzleramt in Vienna.

Nearby tennis, riding, hunting; cable-car to Rax Alps.

2651 Reichenau, Kleinau 34
Tel (02666) 3633
Fax (02666) 363310
Location on southern slopes of Rax; ample car parking
Meals breakfast, lunch, dinner, snacks
Prices rooms SS-SSS with breakfast; reductions for children
Rooms 14 double, 4 single, 1 suite; all have bath or shower, central heating, phone, TV, radio
Facilities 3 dining-rooms, 2 conference rooms, TV room; terrace; gymnasium, health spa
Credit Cards DC, V
Children welcome
Disabled limited facilities
Pets accepted
Closed never **Languages** English, French, Italian
Proprietors Dr Braun, Angela Puskas

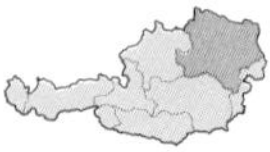

Niederösterreich

Castle hotel, near Zwettl

Schloss Rosenau

This small, baroque mansion, complete with clock tower, nestles in a small wooded valley near the Czech border. It is only 10 km from Zwettl but our inspector needed a good map to find it. Rose bushes and statuary line the approach, while inside every inch of wall space is decorated, every alcove bears a fresco. In contrast, bedrooms are nearly unadorned; some have heavy, dark furniture, others have honey-coloured pine beds, but all have plain white walls. Chef Sonia Etzensdorfer is building quite a reputation for her Waldviertel specialities such as local lamb and game, often combined with berries and mushrooms in the autumn. In the spring, menus include fresh asparagus and shrimp soup and deep-fried elderflowers.

What takes visitors aback, however, is the museum of freemasonry, the only one in Europe. It is an authentic 18thC lodge, complete with symbols and regalia. All quite a contrast to the indoor swimming-pool, mini-golf and tennis courts.

'A classy establishment but not as expensive as one might expect,' read one report. In addition, guests have been impressed by the wheelchair access to five bedrooms.

Nearby fishing, golf, riding, tennis.

3924 Schloss Rosenau, bei Zwettl
Tel (02822) 582210
Fax (02822) 582218
Location deep in country, near Zwettl; ample car parking
Meals breakfast, lunch, dinner, snacks
Prices rooms SS-SSS with breakfast
Rooms 13 double, 4 single; all have bath or shower, central heating, phone, TV, radio
Facilities 3 dining-rooms, TV room, sauna, solarium, indoor swimming-pool
Credit Cards AE, MC, V
Children very welcome
Disabled recommended; 5 bedrooms accessible
Pets welcome
Closed mid-Jan to mid-March
Languages English, French
Managers Gerda Pfauser, Andreas Slechta

Niederösterreich

Village inn, Weissenkirchen

Raffelsbergerhof

A gem, pure and simple. Who would not want to stay in this late-Renaissance house on the edge of the village? Turn off the main street down a little lane towards the Danube and suddenly you are in a flower-filled square. Wistaria and vines climb over this former ship-master's house, where the stables once housed the horses that pulled the Danube barges upstream.

Outside, a statue of St. John of Nepomuk stands in a small niche; inside, a stern stone face spouts water into a tiny pool and ancient steps lead up to reception. Claudia Anton is the second generation of her family to run this pension. Her antique-dealer father restored the 16thC building, then filled it with eye-catching objects. In the breakfast-room, a Biedermeier cabinet displays gold-embroidered *Wachauer Hauben*, the traditional bonnets of the region. Even the locks, handles, hinges and light fittings are finely-crafted and worthy of notice. Views from the vaulted rooms and arcades are either into the garden with its walnut and cherry trees or out towards the late-Gothic church and hills. Bedrooms are attractively-furnished with modern bathrooms; two have views of the Danube.

Nearby church; Wachau Museum.

3610 Weissenkirchen
Tel (02715) 2201
Fax (02715) 220127
Location on edge of village, overlooking square; own car parking
Meals breakfast
Prices rooms SS-SSS with breakfast; reductions for children
Rooms 11 double, 2 single; all have bath or shower, central heating, phone, TV, minibar, radio; some hairdrier
Facilities breakfast-room
Credit Cards MC
Children welcome
Disabled not suitable
Pets accepted
Closed Nov to end April
Languages English, Italian
Proprietor Claudia Anton

Niederösterreich

Village inn, Ysper

Zum Grünen Baum

Many hotels boast of having a 'long tradition of hospitality'; this one offers public proof. A scrolled plaque on the wall bears the date of foundation: 1648. Even without that, the ancient beams, low ceilings, and walls one metre thick bear witness to its age. Not only has this been a coaching inn for all those years, the ownership has passed down through generations of the same family. It could almost be an agricultural museum, with carriage shafts and yokes, rakes and wheels hung on the white-washed walls. The atmosphere, however, is not staid; children are very welcome because 'after all, we're a family ourselves'.

In the *Stüberl*, walls are decorated with embroidered peasant sayings and a target used by hunters for shooting practice. Traditional recipes feature on the large menu, with herbs and vegetables direct from their own garden.

The Rotters have kept up with the times, however, adding a new wing in 1978. Bedrooms here are decorated in light blue, green or grey, with pale pine furniture, compared to the darker look of the older bedrooms. The village, too, is delightfully unspoiled; it even has its own pillory.

Nearby hiking, riding, fishing, tennis, cycling, squash.

3683 Ysper
Tel (07415) 218
Fax (07415) 21849
Location in middle of charming village; car parking on village square
Meals breakfast, lunch, dinner
Prices rooms S-SS with breakfast; reductions for children
Rooms 20 double, 5 single; 3 suites; all have bath or shower, central heating, phone, TV
Facilities 3 dining-rooms, sitting-room, bar, lift/elevator; 2 terraces, garden; sauna
Credit Cards not accepted
Children very welcome
Disabled not suitable
Pets accepted
Closed 2 weeks Feb; 1 week Nov
Languages English
Proprietors Rotter family

Niederösterreich

Village guest-house, Artstetten

Gasthof Landstetter

This cheerful, 100-year old hotel is on a rise above a village famous for its castle. Huge chestnut trees guard the door; bedrooms are large, with majestic views over the countryside. The Landstetters enjoy playing folk-music for their guests.

■ 3661 Artstetten **Tel** (07413) 8303 **Fax** (07413) 8486 **Meals** breakfast, lunch, dinner, snacks **Prices** rooms S-SS with breakfast **Rooms** 28, all with bath or shower, central heating, radio; TV on request **Credit Cards** not accepted **Closed** Jan to Easter **Languages** English

Converted villa, Baden

Pension Almschlössl

Only a 10-minute walk from the middle of the old-fashioned spa of Baden, this Mediterranean-style villa has a large garden with panoramic views of the town. Bedrooms are pretty in pastel blues, with green shutters. Covered garage space.

■ 2500 Baden, Alm 1 **Tel** (02252) 48240 **Meals** breakfast, snacks **Prices** rooms S-SS with breakfast **Rooms** 7, all with bath or shower, central heating, TV **Credit Cards** not accepted **Closed** Nov to Easter **Languages** English

Country mansion, Dörfl

Pedro's Landhaus

This yellow mansion, set in a huge park in the Vienna Woods, is palatial, plush and pricey. Pedro Massana's country club is popular for business meetings and small conferences as well as for gourmet dining. Sauna, tennis.

■ 3072 Dörfl, Kasten **Tel** (02744) 7387 **Fax** (02744) 7389 **Meals** breakfast, lunch, dinner **Prices** rooms SS-SSS with breakfast **Rooms** 11, all with bath or shower, central heating, phone, TV **Credit Cards** MC **Closed** never **Languages** English, French, Italian, Spanish

Castle hotel, Drosendorf

Schloss Drosendorf

A romantic, Renaissance castle where nobility once stayed, this is now in real need of restoration. In a backwater, near the Czech border. Experience rambling rooms, antique and modern furniture, but don't expect to be pampered.

■ 2095 Drosendorf, Schlossplatz 1 **Tel** (02915) 23210 **Fax** (02915) 232140 **Meals** breakfast; small tavern next door **Prices** rooms S-SS with breakfast **Rooms** 21, all with bath or shower, central heating, TV **Credit Cards** not accepted **Closed** last week Dec **Languages** English, French, Italian

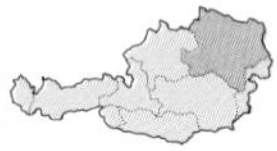

Village inn, Göstling an der Ybbs

Zum Goldenen Hirschen

Next to the Gothic/baroque church, this 550-year old, vine-covered inn is ideal for an overnight stop in this delightful village with its Renaissance houses. The old Stube has chandeliers made of antlers; practical, modern bedrooms.

■ 3345 Göstling an der Ybbs 16 **Tel** (07484) 2225 **Fax** (07484) 222528 **Meals** breakfast, lunch, dinner, snacks **Prices** rooms S-SS with breakfast **Rooms** 18, all with shower, central heating, phone, TV, radio **Credit Cards** V **Closed** never **Languages** English, French

Former medieval house, Klosterneuburg

Hotel Schrannenhof

In the heart of town, the Veit family owns a restaurant, bed-and-breakfast and this small hotel. Carefully converted in 1990, it retains the old arched ceilings and stone floors and has apartments with large bedrooms and small kitchens.

■ 3400 Klosterneuburg, Niedermarkt 17-19 **Tel** (02243) 32072 **Fax** (02243) 3207213 **Meals** breakfast **Prices** rooms SS-SSS with breakfast **Rooms** 13, all with bath or shower, central heating, phone, TV, kitchenette **Credit Cards** DC, MC, V **Closed** never **Languages** English, French, Italian

Old farmhouse, Kronberg am Russbach

Landhaus Kronberghof

The Grossauer family keeps both horse fans and diners happy. With 70 horses and an indoor riding school, there is an authentic rustic atmosphere, deep in the country. Brigitte Grossauer's cooking concentrates on local Weinviertel dishes.

■ 2123 Kronberg am Russbach 3 **Tel** (02245) 4304 **Fax** (02245) 5497 **Meals** breakfast, lunch, dinner, snacks **Prices** rooms S-SS with breakfast **Rooms** 5, all with bath or shower, central heating, phone, TV **Credit Cards** AE, MC, V **Closed** restaurant only, Mon, Tues **Languages** English, French, Italian

Restaurant with rooms, Laaben

Landgasthof Zur Linde

In a charming village in the Vienna Woods, the Stohrs' restaurant is a regular draw for the Viennese who sit in the garden or old Stube. Less well-known are the practical bedrooms in the modern block next door. Special weekend packages.

■ 3053 Laaben 28, im Wienerwald **Tel** (02774) 8378 **Fax** (02774) 837820 **Meals** breakfast, lunch, dinner, snacks **Prices** rooms S-SS with breakfast **Rooms** 14, all with bath or shower, central heating, phone, TV **Credit Cards** not accepted **Closed** Feb, March; restaurant only, Tues, Wed **Languages** German only

Niederösterreich

Restaurant with rooms, Mautern

Landhaus Bacher

Lisl Wagner-Bacher is among Austria's top dozen chefs, so her restaurant, in the middle of a pretty village, is a high temple of cuisine. Rooms in the hotel are very feminine in soft creams and greys. Service may be somewhat haughty.

■ 3512 Mautern, Südtirolerplatz **Tel** (02732) 82937 **Fax** (02732) 74337 **Meals** breakfast, lunch, dinner **Prices** rooms SS-SSSS with breakfast **Rooms** 11, all with bath or shower, central heating, phone, TV, minibar, hairdrier **Credit Cards** DC, V **Closed** mid-Jan to end Feb; restaurant only, Mon, Tues **Languages** English, French

Converted villa, Payerbach

Alpenhof

Architecture fans will appreciate this villa, designed by Adolf Loos 60 years ago. This early example of modern functionalism, with dark-stained wooded furniture, has been altered little. A hideaway for Viennese. Steep approach; dramatic views.

■ 2650 Payerbach **Tel** (02666) 2911 **Fax** (02666) 2670 **Meals** breakfast, lunch, dinner, snacks **Prices** rooms S with breakfast **Rooms** 14, all with bath or shower, central heating; TV on request **Credit Cards** not accepted **Closed** never **Languages** English

❄ Town inn, Puchberg am Schneeberg ❄

Puchbergerhof

Five minutes' walk from the old steam cog railway that goes up the Schneeberg, this 17thC inn is right in town, yet quiet. Ask for a room with a balcony overlooking the garden. Food is filling rather than exciting; vegetarian dishes offered.

■ 2734 Puchberg am Schneeberg, Wiener-Neustädterstr 29 **Tel** (02636) 2278 **Fax** (02636) 22785 **Meals** breakfast, lunch, dinner **Prices** rooms S-SS with breakfast **Rooms** 23, all with bath or shower, phone **Credit Cards** not accepted **Closed** Nov to mid-Dec **Languages** English, some French

❄ Restaurant with rooms, Semmering ❄

Hotel Belvedere

The main draw is not the decoration, but rather the excellent cuisine and welcome from Magda and Karl Engelschall. Desserts in the sunny restaurant are wonderful as the family trained with Demel in Vienna. Large swimming-pool. Ski-lifts 5 minutes.

■ 2680 Semmering, Hochstr 60 **Tel** (02664) 2270 **Fax** (02664) 226742 **Meals** breakfast, lunch, dinner **Prices** rooms S-SSS with breakfast **Rooms** 19, all with bath or shower, central heating, phone, TV, radio **Credit Cards** AE, DC, MC, V **Closed** 2 weeks April **Languages** English, some French, Italian

Niederösterreich

❄ Forest hotel, Semmering ❄

Pension Daheim

This brown, wooden inn with green shutters dates from 1913. Built on a hillside among pine trees, its large terrace has sweeping views of the Rax Alps. Cosy inside, with striking curved banisters, pleasant bedrooms. Viennese-style cooking.

■ 2680 Semmering **Tel** (02664) 2381 **Fax** (02664) 238177 **Meals** breakfast, lunch, dinner, snacks **Prices** rooms S-SS with breakfast **Rooms** 12, all with bath or shower, central heating, phone, TV **Credit Cards** not accepted **Closed** end Oct to mid-Dec; 10 days before or after Easter **Languages** English, French

Modern country hotel, Tullnerbach

Pension Wittman-Wienerwaldblick

An unpretentious, homely retreat in the Vienna Woods, overlooking orchards and valley. The Wittmans are especially hospitable. Decor is rather 1970s, plain and dark. Own lamb, local cheeses on menu. Big terrace. Only 20 km west of Vienna.

■ 3011 Untertullnerbach, Irenental, Brettwieserstr 33 **Tel** (02233) 52147 **Fax** (02233) 521476 **Meals** breakfast, lunch, dinner, snacks **Prices** rooms S-SS with breakfast **Rooms** 7, all with bath or shower, central heating, phone; TV in 2 rooms **Credit Cards** not accepted **Closed** last 2 weeks Nov **Languages** English

Country inn, Weistrach

Landgasthof Kirchmayr

Weistrach is a delightful village and the Kirchmayrs' solid, mustard-coloured country inn is a focal point. As the family's wine-business is just across the street, one hundred wines are on offer in the gourmet restaurant. Some simple rooms.

■ 3351 Weistrach, Haus 9 **Tel** (07477) 42380 **Meals** breakfast, lunch, dinner, snacks **Prices** rooms S-SS with breakfast **Rooms** 4, all with bath or shower, central heating, phone **Credit Cards** not accepted **Closed** one week March; restaurant only, Mon, Tues **Languages** English

Village inn, Ysper

Zur Blauen Traube

In one of Austria's prettiest villages, this typical, pink-painted, Waldviertel inn celebrated its 250th birthday in 1992. Guests dine out in a courtyard full of creepers and geraniums. They also relax in the garden and play skittles in the bar.

■ 3683 Ysper 31 **Tel** (07415) 265 **Meals** breakfast, lunch, dinner, snacks **Prices** rooms S-SS with breakfast **Rooms** 18, all with bath or shower, central heating, phone **Credit Cards** not accepted **Closed** Nov to Easter **Languages** English

Vienna

Area introduction

Vienna

As one of the world's most popular cities for tourists, Vienna is crammed with hotels ranging from 5-star magnificence to the simplest private rooms. All are used year-round, so staff and furnishings are tested to the limit.

Most of the historical and architectural gems, all well-preserved and all well-organised for sightseeing, are within the inner city or along the Ringstrasse. Although the city's heyday was as the capital of the Habsburg Empire, under Maria Theresia and the Emperor Franz Josef I, recent excavations have revealed remains of a Roman military camp. But it is the palaces such as Schönbrunn, Hofburg and the Belvedere that dazzle the eye. Once a visitor has also seen the traditional tourist magnets of the Vienna Boys Choir, the Spanish Riding School and St Stephen's Cathedral, it is time to do what the Viennese enjoy doing most: eating and drinking.

On the fringe of the city are the Heurigen, wine taverns among the vineyards on the edge of the Vienna Woods, just part of the inspiration for Vienna's famous waltz music. In the city itself are the coffee houses, with their dainty pastries.

The most famous hotel is, arguably, the legendary Sacher. Large, lush and home to the rich and famous, the Sacher is opposite the Opera House. Even if you cannot afford to stay here, you can always visit the coffee house to order a slice of the chocolate cake that is synonymous with the hotel.

We have tried to find a range of hotels and bed-and-breakfasts to suit all pockets. As well as the historic hotels in the heart of the city, we have smaller, simpler places to stay. Some are so small that breakfast has to be served in the bedroom, but all fulfil the requirements of cleanliness and personal service that we demand. There is even one inn set amongst the vineyards on the edge of the city, offering the best of both worlds.

In addition to the hotels reviewed in the next 10 pages, for the convenience of our readers, we have also compiled a list of the charming small hotels that are within 80 km/1 hour's drive of Vienna. See the bottom of page 187.

For further details about the city, contact:
Wiener Tourismusverband Vienna Tourist Board, Obere Augartenstrasse 40 A-1025 Wien Tel (1) 211140 Fax (1) 2168492

Telephone numbers
Please note that to telephone Vienna from abroad, the prefix (1) is used. For calls to Vienna from within Austria, the prefix (0222) is required.

This page acts as an introduction to the features of Vienna. The long entries for this state - covering the hotels we are most enthusiastic about - start on the next page. But do not neglect the shorter entries starting on page 134: these are all hotels where we would happily stay.

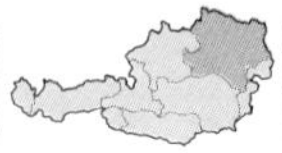

Vienna

Town hotel

Altstadt Vienna

True to form, owner Otto Ernst Wiesenthal has made even more improvements since our first visit. In 1994, he opened up three luxury suites on the second floor. Large by city standards, they can sleep four or five with comfort. Herr Wiesenthal spent 20 years travelling the world, so he knows what he likes and dislikes about hotels. Here, antiques mix harmoniously with modern furnishings in rooms with high ceilings and parquet floors. There is a sense of space throughout, particularly in the seating area which is large enough for a dance routine by Wiesenthal's famous ancestor, Grete, the Isadora Duncan of turn-of-the-century Vienna.

The hotel occupies the upper stories of a wealthy burgher's house in Josefstadt, a well-preserved baroque quarter of the city that is quiet and residential but only 10 minutes by bus from the Ringstrasse. Bedrooms are high enough for roof-top views across to the tower of the nearby St Ulrich's church or towards the western Wienerwald.

You get the feeling that the family enjoy playing host. Nothing seems to be too much trouble, whether it is providing a typewriter a limousine from the airport or concert tickets.

Nearby Ulrichsplatz

1070 Wien, Kirchengasse 41
Tel (1) 52633990
Fax (1) 5234901
Location in attractive street off Burggasse
Meals breakfast
Prices rooms SS-SSSS with breakfast; children up to 6 free in parents' room
Rooms 23 double, 2 single, 3 suites; all have bath or shower, central heating, phone, TV, radio, minibar, hairdrier
Facilities sitting-room, opera and theatre ticket reservations
Credit Cards AE, DC, MC, V
Children welcome
Disabled not suitable
Pets accepted
Closed never
Languages English, Italian
Proprietor Otto Ernst Wiesenthal

Vienna

City hotel

Altwienerhof

Don't be put off by the unfashionable location, south of the Westbahnhof in an unattractive part of town: the Altwienerhof is a gem. Its restaurant, rated one of the best, if not the best, in Vienna, attracts local gourmets as well as foreigners, especially the French. The ever-changing menu focuses on fish, but baby lamb and potato strudel are also specialities; the wine list, with French classics and Austrian vintages, also receives rave reviews.

Chef Rudolf Kellner met his wife in London, where he trained at the Savoy Hotel, and together they have created an atmosphere of intimacy and luxury, both in the alcoves of the restaurant and in the hotel itself.

The best bedrooms echo the *belle époque*, with plush velvet and lace, though gilded taps in the en suite marble bathrooms may be too much for conservative tastes. Note that lower-priced rooms taken with half-pension are a bargain. Breakfast is taken in the conservatory or during warm weather in the garden, sheltered by cascades of ivy.

A warming to those on slimming diets: the smell of delicious food permeates the premises and piques the appetite.

Nearby Haydn Museum.

1150 Wien, Herklotzgasse 6
Tel (1) 8926000
Fax (1) 89260008
Location near Westbahnhof; own garage
Meals breakfast, lunch, dinner, snacks
Prices rooms S-SSSS with breakfast, children under 6 free
Rooms 10 double, 6 single, 4 suites; all with bath or shower, central heating, phone, TV
Facilities dining-room, breakfast-room, conservatory, terrace
Credit Cards AE, DC, MC, V
Children welcome
Disabled not suitable
Pets accepted
Closed never; restaurant only, 1-21 Jan
Languages English, French, Italian
Proprietors Rudolf and Ursula Kellner

Vienna

Wine-village pension

Landhaus Fuhrgassl-Huber

Opened in 1991, this pension immediately made a name for itself among local connoisseurs of small hotels. Set in the long, rather straggly wine-village of Neustift am Walde, it backs on to a slope covered by orderly rows of vines. Here is your chance to drink wine straight from the vineyard of one of Vienna's most famous *Heurigen*, the Fuhrgassl-Huber which just happens to be owned by the same family and is just down the street.

In contrast to the historic *Heurigen*, this hotel is a refreshing combination of old and new. Outside, the cream and white façade is ablaze with azaleas in spring; inside, antique hand-painted peasant wardrobes from the Tyrol catch the eye.

Our inspector enthused about the light and airy atmosphere, created by large windows looking into the courtyard (where guests can breakfast in summer) or out on to the garden. Flowers are everywhere, brightening the natural wood and tiled floors. Bedrooms are generous and comfortable, mainly pristine white, with curtains in clear greens or pinks.

Although central Vienna is only half an hour by bus and tram, the bustle of city life seems further away.

Nearby vineyards, Heurigen villages, Vienna Woods.

1190 Wien, Neustift am Walde, Rathstr 24
Tel (1) 4403033
Fax (1) 4402714
Location on main street of picturesque wine village, outskirts of Vienna; own garage
Meals breakfast, snacks
Prices rooms SS-SSS with breakfast; children under 6 free
Rooms 22 double; all have bath or shower, central heating, phone, TV, minibar, safe
Facilities extended sitting-room, breakfast-room, bar; terrace, garden
Credit Cards MC, V
Children welcome
Disabled reasonable ground floor access **Pets** accepted
Closed 2-3 weeks Feb
Languages English, Italian
Proprietors Krenberger family

Vienna

Suburban hotel

Gartenhotel Glanzing

This is a rarity - an urban hotel catering for families and for business executives. Just outside the middle of the city in the 'green belt', this address is on a quiet, villa-lined street above the castle and park of Pötzleinsdorf. Romy and Wolfgang Kleemann inherited this 1920's cube-like house and turned it into a hotel. Their own Biedermeier furniture adds character to the drawing room, which also has a piano.

With young children of their own, they understand the needs of families, so the garden provides an informal play area and baby-sitting can be arranged. No wonder this is a favourite with embassy staff awaiting permanent accommodation and also with business people accompanied by their families.

Breakfast is buffet-style with plenty of fresh rolls and home-made jams. This is the only meal served but there are plenty of restaurants in nearby wine villages. In addition, the two suites have kitchen facilities as well as private terraces with stunning views across Vienna towards the UNO city. All guests have free use of the small gym, sauna and solarium. Public transport into the city is not on the doorstep; getting into the city is easier by car.

Nearby Pötzleinsdorf Park, Heurigen villages.

1190 Wien, Glanzinggasse 23
Tel (1) 47042720
Fax (1) 470427214
Location on quiet, villa-lined street, private garage but parking no problem
Meals breakfast, snacks
Prices rooms SS-SSSS with breakfast; children under 16 free in parents' room
Rooms 16 double, 4 single; all have bath or shower, phone, TV, radio, minibar, hairdrier
Facilities breakfast-room, TV room, gym, solarium; garden
Credit Cards AE, DC, MC, V
Children welcome
Disabled 1 double; lift/elevator from garage
Pets accepted
Closed never
Languages English, French, Italian
Proprietors Romy and Wolfgang Kleemann

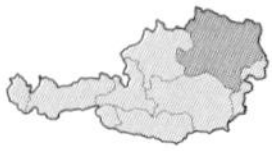

Vienna

Suburban pension

Hotel Jäger

Positive reports continue to come in from readers who have stayed in the suburbs of Vienna with Frau Hartmann and her daughter, who has now come into this 85-year old family-run business. Helene Hartmann knows exactly what a 'charming small hotel' should be, both as hotelier and as guest, having used our guide to Italy on her holidays.

Although Hernalser Hauptstrasse is a main thoroughfare, the 3-storey villa is set back from the road, with lawn and lime trees providing a buffer. Bedrooms on that side are double-glazed, so noise is not a problem.

The lobby features polished wood panelling and a gleaming tiled floor, plus water-colours of 19thC Viennese street scenes. Simplicity is the overall style, though some might call it functional. What makes this bed and breakfast special? The owners, whose welcoming is genuine and whose friendliness is natural.

For longer stays, especially with children, the apartment with its own kitchen is ideal; reserve early for school holidays. Tram number 43 stops opposite the entrance and takes less than half an hour to get to the city centre.

Nearby Heurigen villages, Kongressbad swimming pool.

1170 Wien, Hernalser Hauptstr 187
Tel (0222) 48666200
Fax (0222) 48666208
Location in quiet suburb of Hernals; ample car parking
Meals breakfast, snacks
Prices rooms SS-SSSS with breakfast
Rooms 14 double; 3 single; 1 suite with kitchen; all with bath or shower, central heating, phone, TV, minibar, hairdrier
Facilities 2 breakfast-rooms (1 non-smoking), TV room; garden, terrace
Credit Cards AE, DC, MC, V
Children welcome
Disabled not suitable
Pets accepted **Closed** never
Languages English, French, Italian, Spanish
Proprietors Helene Hartmann, Dr Andrea Feldbacher

Vienna

City hotel

Hotel König von Ungarn

Book well ahead to stay in what many consider the 'jewel in the crown' of Viennese hotels, right in the heart of the old city and only steps away from St Stephen's Cathedral. The present building dates from the 18thC, part of a complex that includes the famous Figarohaus where Mozart composed *The Marriage of Figaro.*

Sitting in the enclosed courtyard, with wood panelling, etched glass and a tree you can imagine yourself back in the days of the Austro-Hungarian Empire. Then, the nobility would stay here for months at a time, attending to courtly duties as well as taking in glittering social events. Some of their portraits line the corridors above, whose windowed galleries are an architectural curiosity. Upstairs, the bedrooms are less glamorous, with the sort of comfortable furnishings found in a private house.

The restaurant, with chandeliers lighting the vaulted baroque ceiling, has a high reputation for traditional Austrian cuisine. At lunch time, it is full of businessmen tucking into boiled beef from the trolley.

The polished service and formal atmosphere does not come cheaply but may be worth it for the 'Viennese experience'.
Nearby St Stephen's Cathedral, Fiaker tours.

1010 Wien, Schulerstr 10
Tel (1) 515840
Fax (1) 515848
Location central; public underground car parking close by
Meals breakfast, lunch, dinner in restaurant
Prices rooms SSS-SSSS with breakfast
Rooms 21 double, 4 single, 8 suites; all have bath or shower, central heating, phone, TV, radio, minibar, hairdrier, air-conditioning
Facilities large atrium courtyard with bar, conference room **Credit Cards** AE, DC, MC, V **Children** welcome
Disabled 1 adapted room, lift/elevator takes wheelchairs
Pets accepted **Closed** never, restaurant only, Sat **Languages** English, French, Italian, Spanish, Portuguese
Manager Christian Binder

Vienna

City hotel

Hotel Römischer Kaiser Wien

Another romantic hotel with a history, this was built as a baroque mansion in 1684 for Johann Hueber, an Imperial counsellor. Later it became a school for engineering under Maria Theresa. Since 1904, it has been owned by the Jungreuthmayer family who have taken care to maintain the old-world flavour of this listed building.

Chandeliers, arches, mouldings, and gilt work have been preserved with newer furniture carefully chosen to blend in with traditional styles. A parlour, with tapestry-covered chairs, provides a useful meeting-place.

Bedrooms come in a variety of sizes and shapes; some have modern furnishings in neutral colours, others are so rich with gold, cream and brocade that 1990's push-button telephones and digital clocks look strangely out of place.

Outside, mischievous carved faces look down on locals and visitors taking time off from shopping and sightseeing at the hotel's pavement café. Annagasse is a narrow street just off the fashionable Kärntnerstrasse, between the Opera House and St Stephen's Cathedral. Arriving by car, use the hotel entrance on Krugerstrasse.

Nearby Staatsoper, Stadtpark, Burggarten, museums.

1010 Wien, Annagasse 16
Tel (1) 515840
Fax (1) 515848
Location in pedestrian area in heart of city, public car park in Beethovenplatz
Meals breakfast, snacks
Prices rooms SSS-SSSS with breakfast
Rooms 24 double, all with bath or shower, central heating, phone, TV, radio, minibar, hairdrier, air-conditioning
Facilities sitting-room, bar
Credit Cards AE, DC, MC, V
Children welcome
Disabled not suitable
Pets not accepted
Closed never
Languages English, French, Italian
Proprietor Dr. Gerhard Jungreuthmayer

Vienna

City hotel

Hotel am Schubertring

No wonder this is a favourite of visiting musicians and artists, who enjoy being on the doorsteps of the Musikverein and the Konzerthaus, with the Staatsoper only a short walk away. Our inspector, an architecture fan, enthuses about the bar, whose mahogany, marble and brass fittings imitate the style of Adolf Loos. Streamlined and rather masculine, this look continues throughout the hotel; there is not a swirling line, frilly curtain, or gilt-edged moulding in sight.

Muted colours ranging from cream and peach to blue and brown are easy-on-the-eye. Bedrooms come in all shapes and sizes, as often happens when old buildings are converted and corridors are long and winding, with sudden turns and changes of level. The staff combines the brisk efficiency of a city hotel with the warmth that attracts families.

Even though it is right on the busy junction of the Ring and Schwarzenbergplatz, rooms are quiet (particularly the suites, each with two bathrooms). Owner Marietta Mühlfellner-Jeannée marks the changing seasons with branches of pussy willow hung with painted eggs at Easter and, of course, a Christmas tree at Yuletide. **Nearby** Staatsoper, concert halls.

1010 Wien, Schubertring 11
Tel (1) 717020
Fax (1) 7139966
Location between the opera house and park on the Ring, corner Schwarzenbergplatz; public car parking nearby
Meals breakfast, bar snacks
Prices rooms SSS-SSSS with breakfast; children up to 6 free
Rooms 30 double, 6 single, 3 suites; all have bath or shower, central heating, phone, TV, radio, minibar, hairdrier, safe, air-conditioning
Facilities lobby, bar, small conference room
Credit Cards AE, DC, MC, V
Children welcome
Disabled 3 rooms with facilities **Pets** accepted **Closed** never **Languages** English, French, Italian, Arabic
Proprietor Marietta Mühlfellner-Jeannée

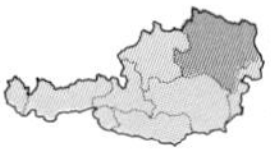

Vienna

City bed-and-breakfast hotel

Hotel Amadeus

No prizes for guessing the theme of this hotel. Some find the cherry-red, white and gold of the furnishings excessive, like the oversweetness of a Mozartkugel; others rate it for location, central and equidistant from all the major sites.

■ 1010 Wien, Wildpretmarkt 5 **Tel** (1) 5338738 **Fax** (1) 533873838
Meals breakfast **Prices** rooms SS-SSS with breakfast **Rooms** 29, all with bath or shower, central heating, phone, TV, radio, minibar
Credit Cards AE, DC, MC, V **Closed** Christmas week **Languages** English, French, Italian

Town hotel

Hotel Attaché

The brutally modern exterior belies the friendly ambience of this hotel, where many staff have worked for years. Sleep in a hand-painted wooden bed or under a dramatic canopy. Popular with business visitors (weekdays) and families (weekends).

■ 1040 Wien, Wiedner Hauptstr 71 **Tel** (1) 5051817 **Fax** (1) 5051817232
Meals breakfast **Prices** rooms SS-SSSS with breakfast; children under 4 free **Rooms** 24, all with bath or shower, central heating, phone, TV, radio, minibar **Credit Cards** AE, DC, MC, V **Closed** never **Languages** English, Italian, Spanish, Portuguese, Russian

Town hotel

Hotel Bajazzo

The extrovert owner, Anne Marie Bogner, exemplifies the mix of nationalities in Vienna; her father is Hungarian and she speaks no fewer than five languages. Practical and modern. Quiet location but close to old city, so handy for sight-seers.

■ 1010 Wien, Esslinggasse 7 **Tel** (1) 5338904 **Fax** (1) 5353997
Meals breakfast **Prices** rooms SSS-SSSS with breakfast **Rooms** 12, all with bath or shower, central heating, phone, TV, minibar **Credit Cards** AE, MC, V **Closed** never **Languages** English, Arabic, Hungarian, Serbo-Croat

Near Vienna

For visitors who prefer to stay near the capital, rather than in it, we list the towns where we have recommended hotels within about 80 km/1 hour's drive of Vienna. Some are in Niederösterreich, listed between pages 105 and 124: Baden, Dürnstein, Klein-Wien, Klosterneuburg, Krems, Laaben, Mautern, Mayerling, Payerbach, Puchberg am Schneeberg, Tullnerbach and Weissenkirchen. The rest are in Burgenland, listed between pages 136 and 142: Eisenstadt, Gols, Mörbisch, Neusiedl and Purbach.

Vienna

City pension

Hotel-Pension Museum

Another pension that harks back to an earlier era. Furnishings are bland, even dowdy, but some bedrooms are enormous, with views of the High Courts and nearby museums. Popular with visiting professors and art lovers.

■ 1070 Wien, Museumstr 3 **Tel** (1) 5235127 **Fax** (1) 523442630 **Meals** breakfast, snacks **Prices** rooms S-SSS with breakfast; children under 6 free **Rooms** 15, all with bath or shower, central heating, phone, TV **Credit Cards** AE, MC, V **Closed** never **Languages** English, French, Italian, Portuguese

City pension

Pension am Operneck

For those on a budget and particularly opera lovers. This is recommended by one reader who bought standing tickets and went every night. Simple, straightforward, clean, and small. Breakfast is served in the bedrooms.

■ 1010 Wien, Kärntnerstr 47 **Tel** (0222) 5129310 **Meals** breakfast in bedroom **Prices** rooms SS with breakfast, children under 6 free **Rooms** 6, all with shower, central heating, phone, TV, radio **Credit Cards** V **Closed** 1 week Feb **Languages** English, French

Suburban villa

Hotel Park Villa

Formerly the Hotel Cottage, this turn-of-the-century villa features huge windows, wrought-iron railings, balconies, and a garden. Favoured by academics visiting the nearby University departments. In the leafy, up-market residential area of Döbling.

■ 1190 Wien, Hasenauestr 12 **Tel** (1) 3191005 **Fax** (1) 319100541 **Meals** breakfast, dinner, snacks **Prices** rooms SSS-SSSS with breakfast **Rooms** 22, all with bath or shower, central heating, phone, TV, radio, minibar, fax point **Credit Cards** AE, DC, MC, V **Closed** never **Languages** English, French, Italian, Portuguese

Burgenland

Area introduction

Burgenland

The easternmost state in Austria is also the least Austrian. Until 1921 it was part of Hungary and life is lived at a slower pace in warmer, drier often dusty weather that produces almonds, figs, apricots and table grapes. But it is grapes for wine that dominate the landscape of the *puszta*, the flat, northern end of the province. As much as one-third of all Austria's wines are produced here. The southern end of the province is wooded, hilly and flecked with castles.

Perhaps the most famous local inhabitants are the storks that nest on the thatched rooftops near the Neusiedl lake, which attracts vast numbers of birds and birdwatchers to the reed beds that ring this unusually warm and shallow inland sea. The lake is also a playground for holidaymakers who take advantage of the constant breezes to wind-surf and sail.

Accommodation is simpler and certainly cheaper than elsewhere in Austria, ranging from modern seaside-style boxes to rooms in old castles. Because the weather is milder and holidaymakers come primarily in the summer, furnishings are more basic.

There are also the *Buschenschenken*, taverns owned by wine-producers to show off the quality of their vineyards. Many have gipsy-style music, as much for tradition as tourism in the area that produced Liszt.

Our inspector was impressed by the Weingut am Spitz in Purbach and the massive castle hotel at Bernstein. As he also loves his music, he recommends visits to towns such as Mörbisch, Lockenhaus and, most of all, Eisenstadt during its annual Haydn Festival in September. Roast goose and red cabbage is the traditional fare on St Martin's Day (November 11) which is celebrated all over Austria, but particularly in Burgenland.

For further details about the area contact:
Landesfremdenverkehrsverband für das Burgenland,
Tourist Board Burgenland,
Schloss Esterhazy,
A-7000 Eisenstadt,
Tel (02682) 63384
Fax (02682) 6338420.

This page acts as an introduction to the features of Burgenland. The long entries for this state - covering the hotels we are most enthusiastic about - start on the next page. But do not neglect the shorter entries starting on page 142: these are all hotels where we would happily stay.

Burgenland

Castle hotel, Bernstein

Burg Bernstein

What do you expect from a castle? This one not only has towers and fortifications, it has a dungeon complete with whipping bench, rack, and cells plus an armoury and an 'Alchemist's Kitchen'. The public can see all this, plus the former Knights' Hall. This is now a restaurant and boasts a splendid early 17thC stuccoed ceiling by Bartolomao Bianco, portraying scenes from Greek mythology. Concerts are held here from time to time. The rest of the castle is for hotel guests.

They enjoy the sitting-rooms, one with ancestral portraits and a lovely baroque tiled *Kachelofen*, another with a huge open fireplace. Even the staircase excites art buffs: it is believed to be designed by Fischer von Erlach, the greatest of Viennese baroque architects.

As for bedrooms, each is different but all are furnished with antiques and are virtually suites. The atmosphere is of yesteryear: no phones, no televisions, no minibars. On cool evenings, wood-burning stoves provide whatever warmth is needed. Some bathrooms are decidedly old-fashioned but these are in some of the most popular rooms, so guests obviously take it all as part of the experience.

Nearby golf, riding, tennis; Bucklige Welt.

7434 Bernstein
Tel (03354) 6382
Fax (03354) 6520
Location in wooded hills above village; car parking in courtyard
Meals breakfast, dinner, snacks
Prices rooms SS-SSSS with breakfast; reductions for children
Rooms 4 double, 5 suites; all with bath
Facilities dining-room, 2 sitting-rooms, bar; terrace, outdoor swimming-pool; sauna
Credit Cards AE, MC, V
Children welcome
Disabled access to ground floor bedroom
Pets accepted
Closed Nov to 1 May
Languages English, French, Italian
Managers Berger family

Burgenland

Wayside inn, Heiligenkreuz

Gasthof Edith Gibiser

Steeply-roofed, thatched cottages are a feature of the flat countryside down here on the Hungarian border, and Edith Gibiser has cleverly incorporated the style into her hotel, or rather her 'hotel complex'.

The Gasthof itself is a solid, square, stone inn complete with terrace dotted with red parasols. Here, the restaurant has a reputation for authentic Pannonian dishes, which have a Hungarian influence, *Zigeuner Fleisch* (a mixture of chicken, beef and pork in a paprika sauce) and herb strudel are specialities.

It is the area behind the inn, however, that captivated our inspector. In the lush meadow that climbs the hillside are new, thatched bungalows that children love to stay in. Each looks like a fairy-tale cabin where Little Red Riding Hood or Snow White would feel at home.

Inside are solid, bright pine beds, tables and chairs with pretty curtains and an individual *Kachelofen.* Parents appreciate the comfort and the modern bathrooms, as well as TV and covered porches for sun-bathing. A nearby *Biotop*, or pond, occupies city children for hours, studying the wildlife.

Nearby Güssing mineral water museum; Schlösslberg; golf.

7561 Heiligenkreuz im Lafnitztal, Hauptstr 81
Tel (03325) 42160
Fax (03325) 424644
Location on Hungarian border; ample car parking
Meals breakfast, lunch, dinner, snacks
Prices rooms S-SSS with breakfast; reductions for children
Rooms 20 double; all have bath or shower, central heating, phone, TV, minibar
Facilities 3 dining-rooms, bar; terrace
Credit Cards AE, DC, MC, V
Children accepted
Disabled not suitable
Pets accepted
Closed 2 weeks Christmas; Feb
Languages English, French, Italian, Hungarian, Slovenian
Proprietor Edith Gibiser

Burgenland

Holiday hotel, Mörbisch

Hotel Restaurant Schmidt

Readers have been agreeably surprised by the standards set by the Schmidt family, here in a part of Austria less visited by western Europeans. They confirm that appearances are deceptive. From the main street of this pleasant, lakeside village with medieval church towers, Das Schmidt looks like just another well-built house. Behind, however, is a modern extension with two tiers of arcades looking on to a large terrace bright with yellow and white sunshades.

Right at the top are the 'Storks' nests'. These six suites are decorated in soft blue and beige, with maple and pear wood furniture crafted by a local carpenter. Large enough for families, they are also suitable for the disabled, with specially fitted bathrooms. The lift/elevator ensures access. The Schmidt family deserve a commendation for their efforts; this is one of the few hotels we have found that takes this provision seriously.

Elsewhere, the furnishings have been renewed but modern stained glass remains a feature. All rooms have views of the lake and there is a play area for children plus a large garden. Herr Schmidt makes his own wine; try his speciality, *Welschriesling.*

Nearby lake, beach; open-air theatre; vineyards.

7072 Mörbisch am See, Raiffeisenstr 8
Tel (02685) 8294
Fax (02685) 829413
Location on main street; own car parking spaces
Meals breakfast, lunch, dinner, snacks
Prices rooms S-SSS with breakfast; reductions for children
Rooms 21 double, 2 single, 6 suites; all have bath or shower, central heating, phone, TV, hairdrier, safe
Facilities 2 dining-rooms, sitting-room; terrace; indoor swimming-pool, health spa
Credit Cards not accepted
Children very welcome
Disabled 6 bedrooms
Pets accepted
Closed Nov to Easter
Languages English, French, Italian
Proprietors Schmidt family

Burgenland

Lakeside hotel, Podersdorf

Gasthof Seewirt

As we have emphasized in the introduction, Burgenland offers simpler accommodation than other parts of Austria. Walter and Marianne Karner have expanded their holiday hotel on the eastern edge of the Neusiedl lake, which has echoes of sea-side Greece or Spain. The Seewirt Hotel has a 1992-built annexe, the Haus Attila and it is here that our inspector feels that families will have an enjoyable holiday. 'The lake view on a hazy day is quite stunning, with sailing boats and windsurfers flickering over the water'. Lawns and poplar trees surround the buildings which have developed from the simple peasant house pictured on the entrance hall wall, dating from 1924.

The third generation of Karners demolished that in 1979 and put up the square, ordinary Seewirt, followed more recently by the Attila. 'Make sure you book into the Attila' is our inspector's advice. Here, the white bedrooms new pine furniture and offer much more space for the blue and white easy chairs and sofas. The food is Pannonian, reflecting the quasi-Hungarian cuisine using local carp, zander and eel, accompanied by Herr Karner's own wines.

Nearby lake, bathing; stork's nests; vineyards.

7141 Podersdorf am See
Tel (02177) 2415
Fax (02177) 246530
Location on lake shore; own car parking
Meals breakfast, lunch, dinner, snacks
Prices rooms S-SSS with breakfast; reductions for children
Rooms 21 double in Haus Attila; all have bath or shower, central heating, phone, TV, radio
Facilities dining-room, sitting-room, TV room; terrace; sauna
Credit Cards not accepted
Children very welcome
Disabled access to bedrooms; lift/elevator
Pets not accepted
Closed Nov to Feb
Languages English, French, Hungarian
Proprietors Karner family

Burgenland

Restaurant with rooms, Purbach

Weingut Am Spitz

Readers who have toured Burgenland confirm that the Am Spitz represents value for money whether you are a wine-lover or not. The owner, Herr Schwarz, has made a success of the vineyards that surround the hotel. His wines, which have won awards in competitions all over Europe, include the gold-medal Blaufränkisch (1992) and silver-medal Cabernet Sauvignon/ Merlot (1992). No wonder the Friday evening meals, complete with a dozen wines, are a great attraction for gourmet weekenders.

The 70-year old restaurant is in what was once the gatehouse of the monastery and is unusually eye-catching, with a voluted baroque façade. All around are lawns studded with chestnut trees, oleanders and ancient stone walls, which make a fine backdrop for summer dining.

Because this is all so attractive, the simple, modern bedrooms in a separate building beyond the car park are a little disappointing. However, the beds are comfortable, bathrooms practical and prices reasonable so we would happily sleep off a fine meal here. Several readers were appreciative of the bedrooms that have been specially adapted for wheelchair users.

Nearby Purbach; lake; cycling, hiking.

7083 Purbach, Waldsiedlung 2
Tel (02683) 5519
Fax (02683) 551920
Location on hill above town; ample car parking
Meals breakfast, lunch, dinner
Prices rooms S-SS with breakfast; reductions for children
Rooms 11 double, 1 suite; all have shower, central heating, phone, TV
Facilities 5 dining-rooms, sitting-room, bar, TV room; terrace, garden
Credit Cards not accepted
Children welcome
Disabled easy access; 2 adapted bedrooms
Pets accepted
Closed Christmas to 1 week before Easter
Languages English, French, Hungarian, Czech
Proprietors Schwarz family

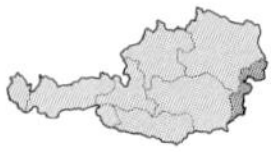

Burgenland

Restaurant with rooms, Eisenstadt

Gasthof-Restaurant Ohr

Johannes Ohr's cooking has made a name for this simple hotel. Austrians flock to enjoy dishes based on asparagus in May, strawberries in June, mushrooms in August and goose in November. Useful stop when touring Burgenland.

■ 7000 Eisenstadt, Rusterstr 51 **Tel** (02682) 62460 **Fax** (02682) 624609 **Meals** breakfast, lunch, dinner **Prices** rooms S-SSS with breakfast **Rooms** 25, all with bath or shower, TV **Credit Cards** not accepted **Closed** March, end Oct **Languages** some English

Restaurant with rooms, Gols

Hotel Birkenhof

A useful stop-over on the way to visit the sights of western Hungary. Enjoy a meal with Helmut Beck's own wines; attentive service, friendly staff. The building is modern and undistinguished. Sunny terrace. Wine-tastings in cellar.

■ 7122 Gols, Festwiese 14 **Tel** (02173) 2346 **Fax** (02173) 242520 **Meals** breakfast, lunch, dinner, snacks **Prices** rooms S-SS with breakfast **Rooms** 21, all with bath or shower, central heating, phone, radio; TV on request **Credit Cards** DC, MC, V **Closed** Mon; 1 month after Ash Wed **Languages** English, French

Castle hotel, Lockenhaus

Burg Lockenhaus

Make sure you reserve a room in the 800-year old castle itself, rather than the large, modern annexe. Behind the towering walls and red-and-yellow shutters are a medieval courtyard, Renaissance stairway, and echoing bedrooms with antique furniture.

■ 7442 Lockenhaus **Tel** (02616) 2394 **Fax** (02616) 2766 **Meals** breakfast, lunch, dinner, snacks **Prices** rooms SS-SSS with breakfast **Rooms** 7 in castle, 41 in annexe, all with bath or shower, central heating, phone, TV **Credit Cards** not accepted **Closed** never **Languages** English

Town hotel, Neusiedl am See

Hotel Leiner

Bird-watchers flock here from all over Europe to spot rare varieties on the Neusiedler Lake. The cheerful welcome offered by Franz and Andrea Leiner also appeals to cyclists. Hearty meals and barbecues in summer. Plain bedrooms.

■ 7100 Neusiedl am See **Tel** (02167) 2489 **Fax** (02167) 248914 **Meals** breakfast, dinner, snacks **Prices** rooms S-SS with breakfast **Rooms** 10, all with bath or shower, central heating, phone, TV, radio **Credit Cards** DC, MC, V **Closed** never **Languages** English, Hungarian; some French

Kärnten

Area introduction

Carinthia

Carinthia is Austria's own Riviera, with the massive Tauern range of mountains protecting the southernmost Federal State from the worst extremes of the weather. A belt of picturesque lakes, running from east to west, provides that Mediterranean feeling, often decorated with resort hotels and promenades. The biggest and most famous is the Wörthersee where the water can reach 28C in summer.

The province has received the European Nature and Environmental Award for the high quality of the water in some 200 lakes across the region. The national parks of the Nockberge and the Hohe Tauern all help to maintain the high standards of cleanliness, so swimming is just as popular as sailing, wind-surfing and boating. Petrol-engines are banned in favour of electric power.

In winter, Carinthia is just as popular, blessed with the sunny, southern slopes of the Tauern as well as the Karawanken range on the Italian and Slovenian borders. As the region has long been a national, as well as an international, playground, the standard of hotel-keeping and restaurants is particularly high.

Bad Kleinkirchheim is a fine example of the quality of the region with its selection of small, family-run hotels. We fell in love with small lakes such as Faakersee as well as the more remote Weissensee lake, the highest in Carinthia, where swimming is popular. Frozen in winter, it is a favourite with the Dutch to engage in their national sport. The road leading up to the Grossglockner, the highest peak in Austria, is impressive in summer and winter, with fine small hotels opening up opportunities to go horse riding in the national forest or to test yourself in downhill skiing.

Klagenfurt, the capital with its old centre, is a pleasant base, with a particularly fine heraldic hall and a renowned hotel.

For further details about the area, contact:
Kärntner Tourismus Gesellschaft,
Carinthia Tourist Office,
Casinoplatz 1
A-9220 Velden
Tel: (04274) 52100
Fax: (04274) 5210050

This page acts as an introduction to the features of Carinthia. The long entries for this state - covering the hotels we are most enthusiastic about - start on the next page. But do not neglect the shorter entries starting on page 158: these are all hotels where we would happily stay

Kärnten

❄ **Chalet hotel, Bad Kleinkirchheim** ❄

Hotel Kapeller

This is the place for golfers, skiers, walkers, and families. There is a practice golf hole behind the hotel with a putting green and sand traps; the 18-hole course is nearby in Bad Kleinkirchheim. Skiers head across the snow to the Nockalm Cable Car in the morning and ski back in the afternoon. Hiking trails abound and as for families, the owners have small children of their own, so their attitude is: the more the merrier. Inside, the layout is open-plan, with no precious, breakable objects; outside there are swings, slides and a hillside to play on.

Bedrooms are furnished in brown but lightened by large windows. There are long bureaux for books, cameras and so on, large wardrobes for sports clothes and deep balconies for privacy. Bathrooms are similarly well-laid out.

Downstairs, everyone congregates around the open fire or in the pale wood-panelled bar. Overall, the hotel is practical and comfortable; the charm is provided by Ingeborg Fritzer, whose young staff are lively, friendly yet always professional. The chef, for example, has to be inventive, since regulars book in for up to 5 weeks during the summer months.

Nearby winter sports; golf, walking trails; thermal baths.

9546 Bad Kleinkirchheim, St. Oswald 72
Tel (04240) 4820
Fax (04240) 48340
Location on hillside, above St. Oswald; ample car parking
Meals breakfast, lunch, dinner, snacks
Prices DB&B SS-SSS for 2; reductions for children
Rooms 16 double, 2 single, 2 suites; all have bath or shower, central heating, phone, TV, hairdrier
Facilities 2 dining-rooms, 2 sitting-rooms, bar, TV room, games room, terrace; sauna, solarium
Credit Cards AE, DC, MC, V
Children very welcome
Disabled not suitable
Pets accepted **Closed** mid-Oct to mid-Dec; mid-April to mid-May **Languages** English, French, Italian
Proprietors Fritzer family

Kärnten

❄ **Resort hotel, Bad Kleinkirchheim** ❄

Hotel Römerbad

Ingrid Putz was an early convert to the benefits of whole-food and organic products. Not only are the breakfast breads baked each morning, the grains are ground just before mixing. "At first my staff and even my family were incredulous; then they saw, and tasted, the difference." Dried fruits, honey, and fruit juices provide sweetness instead of sugar, and only a minimum of butter is used. Although we are wary of whole-food cooking, we were won over by the elegant presentation and delicious flavours produced by award-winning chef, Karl Kaiser. Anyone inspired by these methods can learn the techniques in special classes and take away recipes for use at home. Of course, 'normal' menus are also on offer; there is no pressure to change one's diet.

Similarly, you can do absolutely nothing at all, even though health and fitness are the themes of this hotel. A wide variety of treatments are available and the Kaiserberg ski-lift and Römer thermal baths are only minutes away. Set high on a south-facing hillside, the hotel is open and spacious, with a rather sophisticated ambience. Bedrooms are well-furnished, most have a balcony and there are special *Bio* bedrooms.

Nearby thermal baths; winter sports; hiking, golf, tennis.

9546 Bad Kleinkirchheim
Tel (04240) 82340
Fax (04240) 823457
Location on hill above main road through village; ample car parking
Meals breakfast, midday snack, dinner
Prices rooms SS-SSS with breakfast; reductions for children
Rooms 24 double, 4 single; all have bath or shower, central heating, phone, TV, hairdrier
Facilities 2 dining-rooms, 2 sitting-rooms, bar, conference room; terrace, fitness and health spa
Credit Cards AE, DC, MC
Children very welcome
Disabled not suitable
Pets accepted
Closed 21 April to 21 May
Languages English, Italian
Proprietors Putz family

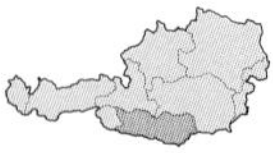

Kärnten

Lakeside hotel, Egg am Faaker See

Kleines Hotel Kärnten

We have received nothing but praise from readers for this contemporary inn. 'To create a hotel to match the view' was the aim of the Tschemernjak family. 'The view' is a panorama across Faaker See to the Mittagskogel rising above other mountains. No wonder when they started as just a bed-and-breakfast in 1972 guests wanted them to serve other meals. "They just didn't want to leave."

Now they stay put and enjoy, for example, hand-made ravioli, leeks from the garden, and lamb with thyme sauce; wines come from small producers, unavailable in the shops. Luise Tschemernjak is in the kitchen, her son is the sommelier, while her husband does everything else. They are locals with extended families: cheese comes from one cousin, another is a butcher.

The hotel is unashamedly modern, with rooms decorated in soft grey and suites in yellow, green, rose or blue. The dining-room, sitting-room, and corridors all boast original works of art, many by a German who came as a child and is now a well-known painter. There are hiking trails and water-sports but many guests, prefer to relax in the garden under the cherry trees, admiring that spectacular view.

Nearby Faaker See.

9580 Egg am Faaker See, Egger Seepromenade 8
Tel (04254) 2375
Fax (04254) 237523
Location in meadows above lake; ample car parking, garage
Meals breakfast, lunch, dinner, snacks
Prices rooms SS-SSSS with breakfast
Rooms 12 double, 4 suites; all have bath or shower, central heating, phone, TV, radio, hairdrier, safe
Facilities dining-room, sitting-room, terrace; garden, own dock and beach
Credit Cards not accepted
Children welcome **Disabled** not suitable **Pets** not accepted
Closed Nov to March
Languages English, French, Italian
Proprietors Tschemernjak family

Kärnten

Restaurant with rooms, Faakersee

Gasthof Tschebull

How do you make a Carinthian feel homesick? Just mention Tschebull, a small hotel with a big restaurant on the edge of the Faaker See. Always open and always busy, this could be written off as just a popular road-side beer-garden and terrace. That would be a mistake. Hans and Willi Tschemernjak are serious chefs, serving up what they call *Alpe-Adria* cooking: a regional style that transcends the nearby borders of Italy and Slovenia.

In the old *Lobiserstub'n*, decorated with Switbert Lobiser woodcuts, we ordered home-smoked eel with home-made rolls, duck breasts with corn dumplings and roast lamb with rosemary gravy, finishing off the meal with walnut ice-cream and hot spice cake with chocolate sauce. The Tschemernjaks not only make ham and sausages, they smoke fish and even distil schnapps. Some guests work off these calories on the tennis courts or by swimming in the lake; others snooze on the private beach.

As for bedrooms, the *Zirbenstub'n* offers affordable luxury, with pale wood, thick moss-green carpets and a sun-room. The bathroom is sumptuous, with glass, brass and pale pink marble plus double wash-basins and a Jacuzzi. Other rooms are simpler.
Nearby lake, woods, hiking.

9580 Egg am Faakersee, Egger Seeuferstr 26
Tel (04254) 2191
Fax (04254) 219137
Location on road, near lake; ample car parking
Meals breakfast, lunch, dinner, snacks
Prices rooms S-SSS with breakfast; reductions for children **Rooms** 12 double, 1 suite; all have bath or shower, central heating, phone, TV, radio
Facilities 3 dining-rooms; terrace, garden
Credit Cards AE, DC
Children very welcome
Disabled access to all rooms
Pets accepted
Closed never; restaurant only, 2 weeks end Jan
Languages English, French, Italian
Proprietors Tschemernjak family

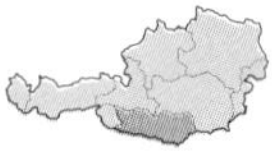

Kärnten

Island hotel, Faakersee

Inselhotel

Half the fun is getting there. Park next to the shore, use the special phone and minutes later, a sleek launch slips into the landing stage. This is the transport to the small island, no more than 100 m wide and 800 m long, that sits in the middle of one of Austria's loveliest lakes; and it all belongs to the Inselhotel.

You can go out just for the day but for the full experience, stay the night. The hotel is some 50 years old, with small dark sitting areas around the reception desk plus a large, square dining-room and terrace overlooking the water. Upstairs, some bedrooms are plain, others have been upgraded and renovated. Bathrooms tend to be white and clinical. Views are of the lake through impressive chestnut trees.

Guests pad about in shorts and bare feet; they play tennis, use the boats, or walk in the woods. Children beg permission to stay the night in the Villa Muh, an old barn near the main building. A nanny keeps small ones amused during July-August. Shore excursions are simple, since the boatman is on duty 24 hours a day. As if on cue, a fawn raced out of the woods and across the lawns just as we were leaving.

Nearby golf, lake, riding, tennis, woods.

9583 Faakersee, Faak am See
Tel (04254) 2145
Fax (04254) 214577
Location on island in lake; ample car parking by ferry boat-house
Meals breakfast, lunch, dinner, snacks
Prices DB&B SS-SSSS; reductions for children
Rooms 17 double, 5 single, 10 suites; all have bath or shower, central heating, phone, radio, safe; TV on request
Facilities dining-room, sitting-room, bar, 2 terraces, games rooms; tennis courts, sailing boats, gardens, beach
Credit Cards not accepted
Children very welcome
Disabled not suitable
Pets accepted, on lead
Closed Oct to April
Languages English, Italian
Proprietors Bucher and Catasta families

Kärnten

❄ Country inn, Feld am See ❄

Hotel Lindenhof

Set beside a splashing fountain and a church, the Lindenhof is at the heart of the quiet lakeside village of Feld am See. Locals still drink in the *Stube*, with its pale wood, bright turquoise seats and deep window sills, crammed with old coffee pots and dolls. Outsiders flock to the 'modern rustic' dining-rooms for award-winning cooking. When our inspectors visited, the menu offered trout cooked with Noilly Prat, steak in a red wine sauce and a rich chocolate terrine. There are also special low-calorie menus.

Comfortable armchairs abound downstairs. Upstairs, the bedrooms in the older building are rather dull, but the newer 'studios', refurbished and expanded in 1990, have extra sitting space, terraces, modern carved country furniture, hyacinth-blue curtains, and bathrooms with lots of shelf space. However, most of them overlook the cemetery.

The Nindlers, whose family have been here for over a century, and have added a fitness room in the basement. The hotel also boasts its own tennis courts and beach on the lake. In winter, cross-country enthusiasts ski around the lake, but the nearest downhill is at Bad Kleinkirchheim.

Nearby lake, tennis; winter sports.

9544, Feld am See
Tel (04246) 2274
Fax (04246) 227450
Location in middle of village; car parking outside
Meals breakfast, lunch, dinner, snacks
Prices rooms S-SSS with breakfast; reductions for children
Rooms 21 double, 4 single, 2 suites; all have bath or shower, central heating, phone, TV, radio
Facilities 2 dining-rooms, 3 sitting-rooms, bar, TV room, terrace; beauty and health farm, own lakeside beach with games **Credit Cards** AE, DC, MC **Children** very welcome **Disabled** not suitable **Pets** accepted **Closed** mid-Nov to mid-Dec; 3 weeks Jan; after Easter **Languages** English, French, some Italian
Proprietors Hermann and Monika Nindler

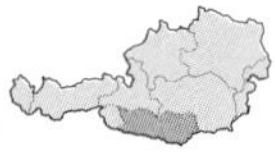

Kärnten

Wayside inn, Grosskirchheim

Nationalparkhotel Schlosswirt

You need time to get the best out of this wayside inn on the famous Grossglockner road. Hubert Sauper has immersed himself in local history and knows all the national park's secret beauty spots. With the help of his wife and family, he renovated the little castle behind the hotel and filled the stables with sure-footed Haflingers. "Dishing up schnitzels and beer is easy on this road. I look for a challenge." So he retraced the steps of the 19thC wine-traders, complete with authentic costume. Now guests can follow part of the same route, go riding, hunting and fishing, or merely admire the wildlife and flowers.

The busy road is quiet when the high pass is closed at night and throughout the winter. The old *Stuben* have the obligatory horns on the walls, but hay-filled cushions and pink tablecloths, too. The food is honest, regional cooking with soup, sausage and cheese always available.

The cheerful bedrooms have plain, solid furniture (made in the village) brightened by cheerful prints. Special events include wine-tastings, Sunday evening dinner in the medieval *Schlössl*, or a torch-lit sleigh-ride.

Nearby local museum; Grossglockner; winter sports, national park.

9843 Grosskirchheim-Döllach
Tel (04825) 211
Fax (04825) 211165
Location on southern side of Grossglockner High Pass; car parking outside hotel
Meals breakfast, lunch, dinner, snacks
Prices rooms S-SSS with breakfast; reductions for children
Rooms 24 double, 4 single; all have bath or shower, central heating, phone; TV on request
Facilities 3 dining-rooms, bar, TV room; terrace, sauna, tennis courts, stables
Credit Cards AE, MC, V
Children very welcome
Disabled not suitable
Pets accepted
Closed usually Nov
Languages English, French, Italian
Proprietor Anton Sauper

Kärnten

❄ **Mountain hotel, Heiligenblut** ❄

Haus Senger

Not many sports stars have turned to hotel-keeping as successfully as Hans Senger, who represented Austria at the 1952 Olympic Games. His small hotel, wedged into a steep hill above Heiligenblut, is a careful mixture of old and new. Rebuilt in 1966, it looks like an old farmhouse thanks to the 400-year old beams and planks rescued from an old barn. These, along with the stone-flagged floors and crackling open hearth, give the dining-room and *Stube* the atmosphere holidaymakers dream about.

Upstairs, most bedrooms are interlinked so they can be used individually or as suites, with connecting doors soundproofed by mattresses. All are decorated in country style with fabrics of soft red, blue or green. Some suites have kitchenettes so parents can make breakfast while the children run around in pyjamas. The *Romantik Zimmer* boasts a four-poster bed painted blue and hung with white muslin curtains.

Menus range from Italian and French dishes to the regular Wednesday fondue evenings. A new wing, with a health and fitness area, blends in cleverly and guests ski out and ski back from a side door. A hotel that is better in reality than in its brochure.

Nearby Grossglockner, winter sports, hiking.

9844 Heiligenblut
Tel (04824) 2215
Fax (04824) 22159
Location off main road above village; ample car parking
Meals breakfast, dinner, snacks
Prices rooms S-SSS with breakfast
Rooms 3 double, 2 single, 8 suites; all have bath or shower, central heating, phone, TV, radio
Facilities dining-room, 3 sitting-rooms, bar, TV room; table-tennis room, gymnasium, sauna, solarium
Credit Cards not accepted
Children very welcome
Disabled not suitable **Pets** accepted but not in restaurant
Closed Oct to mid-Dec; after Easter to mid-June
Languages English, French, Italian
Proprietors Senger family

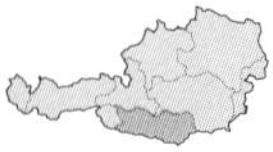

Kärnten

Mountain retreat, Heiligenblut

Villa Kaiser Franz Josef

'Forget the chalets and geraniums, this is totally different from any Austrian hotel I have ever stayed in.' Several readers agree that the Sauper family's 1930s villa is special. Renovated and reopened late in 1993, this has echoes of an English country house. With a maximum of 25 guests, informality is the rule. 'We all call the manageress by her first name, Daniela.'

Although suites are named for Kaiser Franz Josef and his contemporaries, the look is more *House and Garden* than Hapsburg. Instead of ornate furniture and gilt, a few well-chosen antiques are set against plain walls and pale wood floors; even the *Kachelofen* are unusually pretty.

The exception is the Jagd, which reflects the Emperor's favourite sport of hunting with wood panelling and horned trophies. Some rooms boast views of the church and the Grossglockner, Austria's highest mountain.

The Saupers have a special connection with the Kaiser. In 1864, he stayed in their modest hut high on the mountain and granted them the use of his name. Today, this is the Alpenhotel Kaiser Franz Josef, still owned by the family.

Nearby Grossglockner; winter sports; hiking.

9844 Heiligenblut
Tel (04824) 2084
Fax (04824) 208413
Location 3 min walk from middle of village; ample car parking, garage
Meals breakfast, snacks; dinner by request
Prices rooms SSS-SSSS with breakfast; reductions for children **Rooms** 11 suites: all have bath or shower, central heating, phone, TV, *Kachelofen*, minibar, hairdrier, kitchenette
Facilities dining-room/ sitting-room, bar, games room; garden
Credit Cards AE, DC, MC, V
Children accepted
Disabled ground floor access
Pets accepted **Closed** late Oct to early Dec; after Easter to mid-May **Languages** English, Italian, Spanish; some French
Manageress Daniela Fleissner

Kärnten

City hotel, Klagenfurt

Hotel Musil

Sightseers in Klagenfurt's old quarter photograph the Dragon Fountain, the Trinity Column, and the Old and New Town Halls. Those in the know then head for the Musil *Konditorei.* Open every day of the week, it is always busy, with customers queuing for cakes and pastries, plus a dozen sorts of ice-cream. Most of all, however, they ask for chocolates because in this part of Austria, Musil means chocolate.

The *Konditorei* is part of the elaborately-decorated hotel that has been in the Musil family since 1926. The look throughout is pure 19thC. Take a light meal in the inner courtyard, more elegant than any modern atrium. Ornate lights, wrought-iron railings, and a sky-light three floors up provide a setting worthy of ladies in long skirts and hats. The tiny *Stub'n,* full of old guns and trophies from local hunters, serves up smoked salmon mousse, venison cutlets with cranberry sauce and sweet corn dumplings.

Each bedroom is different, but all have a romantic look. You may find a sleigh-bed, a huge gilt mirror, parquet floors, or flowery wallpaper; bathrooms, however, are modern with all the conveniences of a luxury hotel.

Nearby old town; Europapark; Minimundus.

9020 Klagenfurt, 10 Oktoberstr 14
Tel (0463) 511660
Fax (0463) 516765
Location in middle of city; public car parking, garage spaces
Meals breakfast, lunch, dinner, snacks
Prices rooms SSS-SSSS with breakfast; reductions for children **Rooms** 11 double, 1 single: all have bath or shower, central heating, phone, TV, air-conditioning, minibar, hairdrier, safe
Facilities 2 dining-rooms, sitting-room, bar
Credit Cards AE, DC, MC, V
Children welcome
Disabled reasonable access, with lift/elevator
Pets accepted **Closed** Christmas week **Languages** English, some French, Italian
Proprietors Musil Family

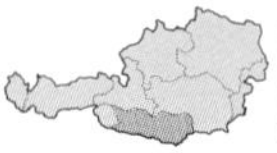

Kärnten

❄ **Town hotel, Kötschach-Mauthen** ❄

Hotel Post

Enthusiastic reports from families with energetic children praise the facilities of this old 'Post' hotel. Every Austrian town has one: some are old and full of character, others are more like barracks with high ceilings and echoing corridors. Here, Margit Klauss shows what taste and imagination can do. Her husband, Wilfried, heads the adventure holiday programme of ski-touring, river-rafting, trekking and fishing which are all carefully graded for age and ability.

Everything is large, from the dining-room with its arched windows overlooking the main street of Kötschach to the children's room with its playhouse and stock of toys. Bedrooms vary: number 14 is a converted attic with dormer windows looking into tree-tops; number 108 has a parquet floor, a sitting area, and a view of the church. In the annexe, chairs and curtains are in matching fabrics and bathrooms are small but adequate. Suites here even have cooking facilities.

Between the old and new buildings is a garden with a heated swimming-pool and fish-pond; the connecting passageway underground leads past a comprehensive health and fitness area.

Nearby local ski area, winter sports, mountains.

9640 Kötschach-Mauthen
Tel (04715) 2210
Fax (04715) 22259
Location in middle of village opposite church; ample car parking
Meals breakfast, lunch, dinner, snacks
Prices rooms SS-SSS
Rooms 21 double, 6 suites; all have bath or shower, central heating, phone, TV, radio; many with hairdrier

Facilities 2 dining-rooms, sitting-room, bar, TV room, games room, 2 terraces; large sauna and health area, heated outdoor swimming-pool, children's room
Credit Cards MC, V
Children very welcome
Disabled not suitable
Pets accepted
Closed Nov, March
Languages English, Italian
Proprietors Klauss family

Kärnten

❄ **Restaurant with rooms, Kötschach-Mauthen** ❄

Sissy Sonnleitner's Kellerwand

Sissy Sonnleitner is a star, voted Austria's 'Chef of the Year' in 1990. Yet she does not work in Vienna, Salzburg, or even a posh ski-resort, but in the village of Mauthen. Find it on the River Gail, a few minutes' drive from the Italian border. Apart from inspiration derived from family holidays in France and Germany, she is self-taught. Her repertoire combines Carinthian and Friuli dishes: she fills pasta Austrian-style, with white cheese, potatoes and herbs but stuffs dumplings Italian-style, with pumpkin.

Kurt Sonnleitner's wine-cellar scores for its competitive prices and wide range of vintages from Italy, Bordeaux, Burgundy and Austria. Breakfast is served under the arches in the peaceful court-yard. The 500-year old *Kellerwand*, with yellow walls and blue shutters, is the oldest building in Mauthen and has been in the family for 90 years. A half-way house for travellers between Venice and Vienna, it merits more than an overnight stay. Those who settle in for a month on half-board are never offered the same dish twice. Bedrooms match the high standards of the cooking: Thonet furniture and Ralph Lauren fabrics with Carrara marble in the bath-rooms.

Nearby alpine and cross-country skiing; fishing, rafting.

9640 Kötschach-Mauthen
Tel (04715) 269
Fax (04715) 37816
Location in middle of village; ample car parking
Meals breakfast, lunch, dinner, snacks
Prices rooms SS-SSSS with breakfast; children under 6 free in parents' room
Rooms 5 double, 5 suites, 2 apartments; all have bath or shower, central heating, phone, TV, minibar
Facilities dining-room, sitting-room, library, bar; terrace, garden
Credit Cards AE, DC, MC, V
Children very welcome
Disabled not suitable
Pets accepted
Closed mid-Nov to mid-Dec; 1 week after Easter
Languages English, Italian
Proprietors Sonnleitner family

Kärnten

❄ **Lakeside hotel, Weissensee** ❄

See-und Gartenhotel Enzian

Our journey up to the Weissensee was worthwhile, since many readers have written in to commend this delightful hotel overlooking Carinthia's highest lake. This provides year-round sport since the water reaches 24° C (75° F) in summer, and freezes in winter, allowing skaters and cross-country skiers to whizz across the snow and ice.

On a dead end road is the Enzian, built by the parents of current owner Herr Cieslar, whose family heirlooms such as clocks, a wedding veil, and photographs add character. The *Enzian* (gentian) theme appears in carvings on shutters and in the blue of tablecloths on the terrace. Inviting armchairs and good reading lamps give the sitting-room the look of a private house, while the well-maintained bedrooms are medium-sized, mainly with white walls and floral curtains.

Where the rest of the hotel is light and airy, the *Almhütte*, just outside, is a dark, cosy cabin that has been converted to a pub, perfect for après-ski or late evening schnapps. Dinner is taken at the Cieslar's larger hotel next door. As well as the garden and clay tennis court, the sailing school is a bonus for youngsters.

Nearby Weissensee, para-gliding, golf, riding; winter sports.

9762 Techendorf am Weissensee
Tel (04713) 2221
Fax (04713) 2305
Location on hillside above lake; ample car parking
Meals breakfast, snacks; lunch, dinner at nearby Ferienhotel
Prices rooms SS-SSSS with breakfast
Rooms 16 double, 3 single, 3 suites, all with bath or shower, central heating, phone, TV
Facilities sitting-room, terrace; garden, tennis court, boats; use of pool, sauna next door
Credit Cards not accepted
Children welcome
Disabled not suitable
Pets accepted
Closed mid-Oct to mid-Dec; mid-March to mid-May
Languages English, Italian
Proprietors Cieslar family

Kärnten

Castle hotel, Wörthersee

Schloss Hallegg

'The best place in the world to have breakfast.' That was the reaction of our inspector who, like all first-time visitors, was open-mouthed at the views. Where else in the world can you sip coffee and munch rolls outdoors on top of castle ramparts? Far below, the land drops away sharply and in the distance, beyond the trees and fields, are the twin towers of Maria Saal.

The castle is approaching its 800th birthday. Built on a rocky outcrop, it is large enough to garrison a small army. Enter the huge portal and you expect to see knights in armour. Instead, roses fill the courtyard and old-fashioned sleds and carriages shelter in the cloisters. Two more stories of arches climb to the steep wood-shingled roof. Everything is on a huge scale, with high ceilings and wood floors. Bedrooms could sleep whole families, while the medieval hall could be a film set. Forty metres long, 9 metres high, with vicious-looking weapons on the wall, it cannot look much different than it did when Otto II of Hallegg lived here. Open only in summer, guests walk in the woods, fish on the private lake, play tennis, and peep into the tiny chapel in the tower, big enough for only two pews.

Nearby lake, tennis, woods, fishing, riding.

9061 Krumpendorf am Wörthersee, Halleggerstr 131
Tel (0463) 49311
Fax (0463) 493118
Location in woods, high above Krumpendorf; ample car parking
Meals breakfast
Prices rooms SS-SSS with breakfast; reductions for children
Rooms 15 double; all have bath or shower, central heating, phone, TV, radio, minibar
Facilities dining-room, sitting-room; tennis court
Credit Cards not accepted
Children very welcome
Disabled not suitable
Pets accepted
Closed Oct to mid-May
Languages some English
Proprietor Frau Melita Helmigk

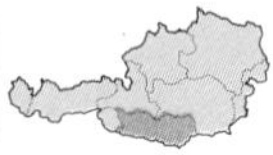

Kärnten

❄ Mountain hotel, Afritz ❄

Hotel Lärchenhof

The Tronigger family is sports-mad as the array of trophies shows. Families spend time on the three tennis courts, in the swimming-pool and hiking. In winter, they ski straight from the door. Public rooms and bedrooms are plain.

■ 9542 Afritz-Verditz **Tel** (04247) 2134 **Fax** (04247) 213411
Meals breakfast, lunch, dinner, snacks **Prices** DB&B S-SS **Rooms** 23, all with shower, central heating, phone **Credit Cards** not accepted
Closed Oct to mid-Dec; after Easter to early May **Languages** English

❄ Mountain resort hotel, Bad Kleinkirchheim ❄

Hotel Kaiserburg

Tucked between private houses on the Kaiserburg side of the main road, the ski lifts are virtually at the door, the thermal baths just a 5-minute walk. Indoor swimming-pool overlooks the garden. A jolly ambience thanks to the Hermann family.

■ 9546 Bad Kleinkirchheim **Tel** (04240) 365 **Fax** (04240) 3658
Meals breakfast, lunch, dinner, snacks **Prices** rooms S-SSS with breakfast **Rooms** 27, all with bath or shower, central heating, phone
Credit Cards not accepted **Closed** Nov to mid-Dec; short period after Easter **Languages** English, Italian

❄ Village hotel, Bad Kleinkirchheim ❄

Hotel Sonnalm

Quiet location at the end of the village and just a stone's throw from lift connections to the Nockalm and Maibrunn-Kaiserburg systems. Modern, above average comfort. Huge picture windows in the spacious sitting and dining-rooms. Large garden.

■ 9546 Bad Kleinkirchheim **Tel** (04240) 507 **Fax** (04240) 8505
Meals breakfast, dinner, snacks **Prices** DB&B SS-SSS **Rooms** 24, all with bath or shower, central heating, phone, TV, radio **Credit Cards** not accepted **Closed** April (depending on Easter); Nov to mid-Dec
Languages English, Italian, some French

Farmhouse hotel, Diex

Berggasthof Jesch

Tucked into the south-eastern corner of Carinthia, Diex is one of the sunniest villages in Austria. The Jesch family farm provides horse-riding as well as fresh produce for the table. Suitable for children. Rural simplicity.

■ 9103 Diex, Wandelitzen 10 **Tel** (04232) 7196 **Fax** (04232) 719620
Meals breakfast, lunch, dinner, snacks **Prices** rooms S-SS with breakfast
Rooms 22, all with bath or shower, central heating, phone, TV
Credit Cards not accepted **Closed** Nov to April **Languages** English

Kärnten

Country inn, Faaker See

Bernold's Landhotel 'Gasthof Post'

Old-fashioned and rather dark inside but brightened by the enthusiasm of Herr Bernold, who has expanded his hotel into a mini-empire with restaurant, night-club, bistro, tennis courts and private beach nearby. Also owns Villa Faakersee across the street.

■ 9580 Drobollach am Faaker See, Seeblickstr 47 **Tel** (04254) 2184 **Meals** breakfast, lunch, dinner, snacks **Prices** rooms S-SS with breakfast **Rooms** 30, all with bath or shower, central heating, phone, TV, radio, minibar, safe **Credit Cards** AE, DC **Closed** never **Languages** English

❄ Mountain guest-house, Feld am See ❄

Gasthof-Pension Hubmannhof

Quiet location on hillside with view of Feld am See and valley. In summer, chickens scratch for food, hay dries in the meadow, and guests take the sun on the terrace, walk and enjoy water sports. Simple, clean and inexpensive.

■ 9544 Feld am See, Wiesen 8 **Tel** (04246) 2667 **Fax** (04246) 228078 **Meals** breakfast, dinner, snacks **Prices** DB&B S-SS **Rooms** 10, most with bath or shower, central heating **Credit Cards** not accepted **Closed** never **Languages** English

Town hotel, Friesach

Friesacherhof

Friesach, with its moat and old walls, is Carinthia's oldest town and well worth exploring. Alfred Pötscher's simple hotel is on the ancient main square near the famous fountain. Rooms at the front have a splendid view, but lack sound-proofing.

■ 9360 Friesach, Hauptplatz 4 **Tel** (04268) 2123 **Fax** (04268) 212315 **Meals** breakfast, lunch, dinner, snacks **Prices** rooms S-SS with breakfast **Rooms** 15, all with bath or shower, central heating, phone, TV **Credit Cards** AE, DC, MC, V **Closed** never **Languages** English

❄ Wayside inn, Grosskirchheim ❄

Hotel Post

At the southern end of the Grossglockner Pass, in the heart of the Hohe Tauern National Park, Franz-Josef Sauper's yellow-painted hotel is popular with hikers in summer. Skiers go to Heiligenblut in winter. Pleasant garden; modern health spa.

■ 9843 Grosskirchheim **Tel** (04825) 205 **Fax** (04825) 20519 **Meals** breakfast, lunch, dinner, snacks **Prices** rooms S-SS with breakfast **Rooms** 28, all with bath or shower, central heating, phone, TV **Credit Cards** AE, DC, V **Closed** 2 weeks after Easter **Languages** English

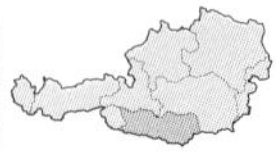

Kärnten

Country hotel, Ledenitzen

Restaurant-Pension Forellenhof

A jolly, family and sports-oriented hotel with huge swimming-pool and tennis courts near Faakersee. Big breakfasts and hearty dinners are chef Helmut Kerschbaumer's specialities. Try the trout and venison, then indulge in home-made cakes.

■ 9581 Ledenitzen, St Martinstr 16 **Tel** (04254) 2371 **Fax** (04254) 4078 **Meals** breakfast, lunch, dinner **Prices** rooms S-SS with breakfast **Rooms** 28, all with bath or shower **Credit Cards** AE, MC, V **Closed** Mon (Oct-Apr); Jan, Feb **Languages** some English, some Italian

Lakeside hotel, Millstatt am See

Hotel Hubertusschlössl am See

Only a lawn separates this 19thC house, with romantic tower, from the Millstättersee. Choose Room 24 for its balcony and summertime view of boats and windsurfers. The Hohenwarter-Sodek family also own the modern Hotel Seewirt nearby.

■ 9872 Millstatt am See, Kaiser-Franz-Josef-Str **Tel** (04766) 2110 **Fax** (04766) 211054 **Meals** breakfast; lunch, dinner at Hotel Seewirt **Prices** rooms S-SSS with breakfast **Rooms** 18, all with bath or shower, central heating, phone, minibar, radio; some TV **Credit Cards** AE, DC, MC, V **Closed** Oct-Apr **Languages** English, French, Italian

Health farm, Millstättersee

Biohotel Alpenrose

The Obweger's inn is recognized as Austria's first Biohotel, setting the trend for organic food, health-conscious diets and rooms furbished in natural materials like wood and cotton. Overlooks Millstättersee lake. Outdoor swimming-pool.

■ 9872 Millstatt am See, Obermillstatt 84 **Tel** (04766) 2500 **Fax** (04766) 3425 **Meals** breakfast, dinner, snacks **Prices** DB&B from SS for 2 **Rooms** 27, all with bath or shower, central heating, phone, TV **Credit Cards** not accepted **Closed** first 2 weeks Dec; last 2 weeks Jan **Languages** English, French, Italian

Guest-house, Ossiach

Naturgasthof-Schlosswirt

Known for its organic cooking, using free-range farm produce. Sit outside under gold and white striped umbrellas and order coffee and home-made cakes. Plain, unpretentious and inexpensive, some rooms have a lake view. Private dock.

■ 9570 Ossiach 5 **Tel** (04243) 8747 **Meals** breakfast, lunch, dinner, snacks **Prices** rooms S-SS with breakfast **Rooms** 6, all with bath or shower, central heating **Credit Cards** not accepted **Closed** Nov to April **Languages** English, Italian

Kärnten

Village inn, Paternion

Gasthof Tell

A useful overnight halt to experience a jolly 700-year old inn in the Drau valley. The enthusiasm of the Michorl family makes up for the old-fashioned furnishings. Carinthian dishes are a speciality in the busy Stube. Dancing in the cellar-bar.

■ 9711 Paternion **Tel** (04245) 2931 **Fax** (04245) 3026 **Meals** breakfast, lunch, dinner, snacks **Prices** rooms S with breakfast **Rooms** 18, all with bath or shower, central heating, phone, TV **Credit Cards** MC, V **Closed** 2 weeks Oct **Languages** English, French

Restaurant with rooms, Ruden

Gasthof Pfau Obstgut

Eat, sleep and wander round the orchards where some of Austria's most famous *Schnaps* is made. Valentin Latschen's restaurant enjoys a burgeoning reputation. Renovated bedrooms in the century-old building, more in a modern extension.

■ 9113 Ruden, Untermitterdorf 1 **Tel** (04234) 8221 **Fax** (04234) 8220 **Meals** breakfast, lunch, dinner **Prices** rooms S-SS with breakfast **Rooms** 7, all with bath or shower, central heating **Credit Cards** AE, DC, MC, V **Closed** Jan to March; restaurant only, Mon, Tues in April, Oct-Dec **Languages** English

Town hotel, St Veit an der Glan

Hotel Mosser

St Veit is such an historic town that it deserves better accommodation. In a quiet side street, the Mosser has plain bedrooms above a modern bar and restaurant. Adequate as a base to explore the medieval squares and fortifications.

■ 9300 St Veit/Glan, Spitalgasse 6 **Tel** (04212) 3223 **Fax** (04212) 322310 **Meals** breakfast, lunch, dinner, snacks **Prices** rooms S-SS with breakfast **Rooms** 15, all with bath or shower, central heating, phone, TV **Credit Cards** not accepted **Closed** never **Languages** English

Lakeside hotel, Wörthersee

La Promenade

Parisian chef Ervé Delclos and his Austrian wife, Ulrike, opened this quiet hotel eight years ago. They deliberately omit both phone and TV from the bedrooms, so guests really can relax. Classic French sauces in the restaurant. Well-priced comfort.

■ 9201 Krumpendorf am Wörthersee, Strandpromenade 5 **Tel** (04229) 2763 **Fax** (04299) 3784 **Meals** breakfast, dinner, snacks **Prices** rooms S-SSS with breakfast **Rooms** 15, all with bath or shower, central heating **Credit Cards** AE, MC, V **Closed** 3 weeks Oct; 2 weeks Feb **Languages** English, French

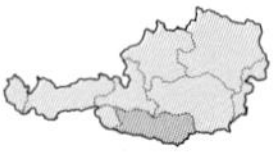

Kärnten

Lakeside villa, Wörthersee

Villa Riva

Right on the water, with statues on the lawn, the former summer home of King Alfonso XIII of Spain remains both luxurious and exclusive. Apartments only, and furnished like a private house. Most guests in high season stay a minimum of 2 weeks.

■ 9210 Pörtschach, Wörthersee, Haupstr 293 **Tel** (04272) 32100 **Fax** (04272) 321747 **Meals** breakfast, lunch **Prices** rooms SSS-SSSS, with breakfast **Rooms** 16, all with bath or shower, central heating, phone, TV, minibar, kitchenette **Credit Cards** not accepted **Closed** Oct to April **Languages** English, French, Italian

Lakeside villa, Pörtschach am Wörthersee

Seehotel Frech

Although Dr Claudia Brugger has converted her parents' elegant summer-house into a bed-and-breakfast, it still looks and feels like a private home. Right on the water, with its own dock; protected from the road by a large garden.

■ 9210 Pörtschach am Wörthersee, Töschling 80 **Tel** (04272) 2447 **Fax** (04272) 244717 **Meals** breakfast **Prices** rooms SSS with breakfast **Rooms** 6, all with bath or shower, phone, TV **Credit Cards** not accepted **Closed** Oct to April **Languages** English

Lakeside hotel, Velden am Wörthersee

Seehotel Tropic

The Wenger family want everyone to have fun at this attractive hotel that is the width of a lawn away from the water. The lake-side café, dock and boats are all part of their 'Beach Club' that attracts younger visitors.

■ 9220 Velden, Klagenfurterstr 40 **Tel** (04274) 20370 **Fax** (04274) 203742 **Meals** breakfast, lunch, dinner, snacks **Prices** rooms S-SSSS with breakfast **Rooms** 14, all with bath or shower, central heating, phone, TV, radio, minibar, safe **Credit Cards** not accepted **Closed** never **Languages** English, French

Steiermark

Area introduction

Styria

Styria advertises itself as the 'Green Heart of Austria' and certainly has miles of unspoilt countryside. As the second-largest state, it also has large variations of landscape, ranging from the Totes Gebirge, the Dead Mountains in the north-west, to the flat plains in the east; rolling hills in the south are covered in vineyards, whilst the Dachstein range is a skier's and climber's delight.

Small, family-run hotels abound for holiday-makers, many emphasising that they are environmentally-friendly. This is apple country, with one or two small hotels that offer apple cures, claiming that an apple a day can do things for you that even teachers rarely experience. As the province is so large, there are more sophisticated places to stay in the extreme west, round Altaussee and Gröbming, as well as hideaways for winelovers in Kapfenstein and Kitzeck which deserve time in order to savour the renaissance of Austrian winemaking.

Graz, the state capital, is rather under-rated, but well worth spending time in to explore its old streets, Schloss Eggenberg, one of Europe's largest collections of medieval arms and a thriving cultural life epitomised by the Styriarte (a classical music festival) in July and the Styrian Festival in October.

On the high sunny plain near Ramsau, mountaineering is a holiday activity on offer, with instruction by your hotelier, an acknowledged expert. The choices are there, with inns to match, for everyone and anyone, whether they are looking for peace and quiet or healthy activity.

For further details about the area contact:
Steirische Tourismus,
Styrian Tourist Office,
St Peter Hauptstrasse 243,
A-8042 Graz-St Peter
Tel (0316) 4030330
Fax (0316) 40303310

This page acts as an introduction to the features of Styria. The long entries for this state - covering the hotels we are most enthusiastic about - start on the next page. But do not neglect the shorter entries starting on page 179: these are all hotels where we would happily stay.

Steiermark

❄ Converted hunting lodge, Altaussee ❄

Hubertushof

'One of a kind' was our reaction, after a tour with the owner, Countess Strasoldo-Graffemberg. Most Austrian inns have a few hunting trophies on the wall; here there are hundreds, in the entrance hall, above the stairs and in the corridors. Many pre-date the house, built in 1894 for the Countess's grandparents. The atmosphere of yesteryear remains, but without the gloom of some old buildings. It still looks and feels like a private home where guests are invited, rather than paying, to stay. In the sitting-room, a grandfather clock ticks loudly opposite an open fire; a hand-written note on the desk announces that the bar is open from 5.30-7 pm.

From the terrace, the picture-postcard vista of the lake is enchanting, with the Loser and Trisselwand mountains as a backdrop. Above is the private balcony of the suite, 'one of the prettiest I've ever seen' and dazzlingly white with highlights of blue. Room four, a total contrast, is a bold combination of royal blue and cherry red; number three has painted country furniture. The hospitality extends to details: a box of tissues, a shoe horn and a nail file set out on a table, a lap-rug on a *chaise-longue*.

Nearby Altaussee lake; Loser cable-car; winter sports.

8992 Altaussee, Puchen 86
Tel (03622) 71280
Fax (03622) 7128080
Location on hillside above village; ample car parking
Meals breakfast
Prices rooms SS-SSS with breakfast
Rooms 4 double, 2 single, 3 suites; all have bath or shower, central heating, phone; some TV
Facilities breakfast-room, sitting-room, bar; terrace, garden
Credit Cards AE, MC, V
Children welcome
Disabled not suitable
Pets accepted
Closed mid-Oct to 26 Dec; 11 Jan to 1 Feb; March, April, May; open at Easter **Languages** English, some French, Italian
Proprietors Countess Rosemarie Strasoldo-Graffemberg

Steiermark

❄ Lakeside hotel, Altaussee ❄

Hotel Seevilla

What was a rather sombre and old-fashioned looking hotel in the early 1990s has been overhauled. Readers approve of the light, airy dining-room, with picture windows overlooking lake and lawns. They have not complained about the significant increase in size. Built in 1978, the Seevilla stands among summer homes where the road dead ends at the water. Modern comforts now include an glamourous indoor swimming-pool with the usual sauna and massage facilities. Families like the attic bedrooms, with the pale wood beams and rooftop views.

This resort was a favourite of composers and writers in the 19thC. Arthur Schnitzler and Gustav Mahler visited; so did Brahms, whose Piano Trio in C Major, Opus 87 and Spring Quintet in F Major, Opus 88, were played for the first time in a house on this site. Classical music evenings continue the tradition. Outside, not much has changed here by the Altaussee; lilacs still bloom in spring while the birch and ash, chestnut and maple trees provide shade from summer sun. Ducks waddle to the water, plunge in and swim out towards the moored sailboats. At the far end of the lake, granite cliffs drop down to the water.

Nearby lake, golf, tennis, hiking, fishing; winter-sports

8992 Altaussee
Tel (03622) 71302
Fax (03622) 713028
Location at end of lane on lake; ample car parking
Meals breakfast, lunch, dinner, snacks
Prices rooms SS-SSSS with breakfast
Rooms 40 double, 7 single, 6 suites; all have bath or shower, central heating, phone, TV, minibar, hairdrier
Facilities 2 dining-rooms, sitting-room; terrace; indoor swimming-pool, sauna, fitness area; garden, dock
Credit Cards AE, DC
Children welcome **Disabled** reasonable access; lift/elevator
Pets accepted, not in dining-room **Closed** mid-Oct to mid-Dec; 2 weeks after Easter
Languages English
Proprietors Maislinger-Gulewicz family

Steiermark

Castle hotel, Deutschlandsberg

Burg Hotel Deutschlandsberg

There is a certain thrill about staying in a castle, which is why readers have alerted us to this medieval pile that dominates the attractive village of Deutschlandsberg, deep in the country. With its drawbridge and foreboding gateways, there are still echoes of the battles fought centuries ago with the Turks and Hungarians.

Once inside the massive walls, however, there is surprising comfort. Gert Schick, who comes from a family of hoteliers, and his wife Karin, who is a qualified dentist, bought the fortress back in 1989 and turned it into a meeting place for locals as well as tourists. In 1994, they completely redecorated the bedrooms, putting in the conveniences demanded by international travellers. Although there are some antiques, most of the furniture is refreshingly simple. Some rooms boast hand-painted country furniture, others have more contemporary fabrics. The restaurant, once the Rittersaal or Knights Hall, is impressive, with a massive beamed ceiling. The bar has a history of its own, since it once graced the Steirerhof Hotel, a landmark in Graz. Despite the veneer of history, the Schicks ensure that guests relax and enjoy their unusual surroundings.

Nearby cycling, fishing, golf, riding, tennis.

8530 Deutschlandsberg, Burgstr 19
Tel (03462) 5656
Fax (03462) 565622
Location overlooking village; ample car parking
Meals breakfast, lunch, dinner, snacks
Prices rooms S-SSS with breakfast; reductions for children
Rooms 15 double, 2 single, 6 suites; all have bath or shower, central heating, phone, radio, TV, minibar
Facilities 2 dining-rooms, sitting-room, dance bar, seminar rooms; terrace; health and fitness area
Credit Cards not accepted
Children welcome
Disabled not suitable
Pets accepted
Closed Jan to March
Languages English, French
Proprietors Schick family

Steiermark

❄ Country hotel, Etmissl ❄

Etmissler Hof

'From the balcony, you can watch the moon rise twice, on either side of the Hochschwab', wrote our inspector on his visit to this wayside inn. Find it at the end of the road in the hamlet of Etmissl, which itself is at the end of a peaceful valley where pine forests cover rolling hills. The hotel dates from 1788; the Wöls family took over in the 19thC.

Anna Wöls is the sort of owner who is keen for all her guests to enjoy their stay. During the main holiday season there is a daily programme of supervised children's activities, ranging from tractor rides to evening campfires. There is table-tennis, an outdoor, heated swimming-pool, plus a separate building where youngsters can make as much noise as they like. They can play safely in the surrounding meadows, help the chef cook spaghetti and then congregate at their own table for dinner. No wonder it is a well-known member of Austria's children's hotels group: parents can sit back, relax and recharge their own batteries while the younger generation happily wear down theirs. This is popular with people from the UNO city in Vienna who want the outdoor life (skiing and hunting) but plenty of creature comforts.

Nearby hiking; winter sports; Grünersee; Mariazell church.

8622 Etmissl
Tel (03861) 8110
Location at end of lovely valley; ample car parking
Meals breakfast, lunch, dinner, snacks
Prices rooms S-SSS with breakfast; reductions for children **Rooms** 25 double, 5 single; all have bath or shower, central heating, phone, radio, minibar; TV on request
Facilities 3 dining-rooms, 2 sitting-rooms, reading-room, bar, 2 TV rooms, table-tennis; 2 terraces, gymnasium, health spa, outdoor swimming-pool, garden, tennis, bicycles
Credit Cards AE, DC, MC, V
Children very welcome
Disabled not suitable
Pets accepted
Closed 10 to 25 Jan
Languages English, French
Proprietors Wöls family

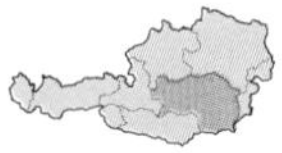

Steiermark

Town inn, Feldbach

Landgasthof Herbst

Johann Herbst is the fourth generation of the family to run this wayside inn in the heart of Styria. The pink-painted, rather modern-looking hotel is through a medieval gateway with a big garden behind, crammed with fruit trees and children's climbing frames. Although the renovations were back in 1988, the interior still looks fresh throughout, mostly in spruce wood which shows the grain, or elegant cherry-wood. The older rooms have oak furniture, cream walls and pink or beige materials.

All this is merely a backdrop for the enthusiastic Herbst family whose restaurant is renowned for its Styrian specialities, which range from smoked ham and meat strudel to trout and 'gentleman's goulash'. They will even provide an 'English breakfast' with eggs for visitors feeling home-sick.

The clientele includes businessmen during the week; otherwise, families with small children enjoy the safety of the garden as well as the indoor swimming-pool at the town's leisure centre 200 m away. All in all, we rate this as a very professionally-run place and applaud the specially-adapted bedrooms for disabled guests.

Nearby fortifications, pumpkin-seed oil museum; Schloss Kornberg; cycling, hiking.

8330 Feldbach, Gniebing 15
Tel (03152) 2741
Fax (03152) 274130
Location on main road, just outside town; car parking outside
Meals breakfast, lunch, dinner, snacks
Prices rooms SS-SSS with breakfast; reductions for children
Rooms 17 double, 5 single, 1 suite; all have bath or shower, central heating, phone, TV
Facilities 4 dining-rooms, 2 sitting-rooms, bar, table-tennis room; 2 terraces, garden
Credit Cards AE, DC, MC, V
Children very welcome
Disabled easy access, 3 bedrooms adapted
Pets accepted; not in restaurant **Closed** 22 Dec to 15 Jan **Languages** English, French, Italian
Proprietors Herbst family

Steiermark

Town hotel, Graz

Schlossberg Hotel

We include this hotel despite the fact that it has well over 30 bedrooms. Our roving reporter, who has long had a love affair with Graz, was insistent: 'We must include somewhere nice to stay in Graz; this is extraordinarily elegant and it does maintain the charming, small ambience we want'.

Vivid blue, with black shutters, this amalgamation of two 15thC bourgeois houses could not be better placed. Step off the embankment and back in time. The hotel's entrance hall retains its stout pillars and vaulted ceiling. Everywhere antique furniture maintains the sense of history, thanks to Frau Marko's excellent taste, acquired as an antiques dealer. A gilded sconce, like an arm, holds two candles near the reception desk.

Under the exposed beams, a cuddly, cross-eyed gilded lion's head greets visitors who, like our inspector, covet the genuine Biedermeier settee. The only blemish is the bar area, where the modern, leather furniture is somewhat garish. The bedrooms, however, are carefully furnished, often with whitewashed walls and even more antiques. There is a roof-garden with views over the Styrian capital.

Nearby Schlossbergbahn, cathedral; Weapons Museum.

8010 Graz, Kaiser-Franz-Josef-Kai 30
Tel (0316) 80700
Fax (0316) 807070
Location on river, below Schlossberg; own car parking, garage
Meals breakfast
Prices rooms SSS-SSSS with breakfast; reductions for children
Rooms 37 double, 14 single, 4 suites; all have bath or shower, central heating, phone, TV, radio, minibar
Facilities sitting-room, bar; terrace, outdoor swimming-pool; gymnasium, sauna
Credit Cards AE, DC, MC, V
Children welcome
Disabled not suitable
Pets accepted
Closed Christmas **Languages** English, French, Italian
Manageress Frau Gfrerer
Proprietors Marko family

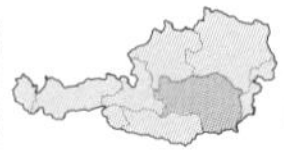

Steiermark

❄ **Country inn, Gröbming** ❄

Landhaus St. George

This is a favourite with our readers, due partly to its position and partly to the owners, who have a strong sense of humour. "I'm just a jack of all trades," says Kurt Langs, his keen blue eyes alight with self-mockery. Back in 1973, he made a career change, found an empty hillside and built the hotel with his own hands. Two years later, he and his wife opened their inn, with only four rooms. Since then, gradual expansion has resulted in first-rate comforts and a clever blending of old and new wood. Here is proof that 'modern' need not mean characterless squares and rectangles.

Take the *Georgstub'n*. A circular table fits neatly into the large bay window, whose shape is echoed by the octagonal bar. Deep red Persian carpets and green tapestry cushions provide colour against a background of knotty pine. Bedrooms are generously-sized and named for the mountain in view, such as Freispitz and Freienstein. Despite the plush furnishings, no eyebrows are raised when hikers return with boots and backpacks. That is because Herr Langs is also a mountain climber, who has notched up over 1,500 hikes with his guests. In winter, a beginners' slope and ski-school are only 600 m away.

Nearby Stoderzinken mountain; winter sports; hiking, climbing.

8962 Gröbming 555
Tel (03685) 22740
Fax (03685) 2274060
Location on quiet hillside above private road; ample car parking, garage
Meals breakfast, dinner, snacks
Prices DB&B SS-SSS; reductions for children
Rooms 10 double, 12 suites; all have bath and shower, central heating, phone, TV, hairdrier, safe
Facilities 2 dining-rooms, bar; conference room, indoor swimming-pool, sauna, steambaths; terraces, garden
Credit Cards AE, DC, MC, V
Children very welcome
Disabled limited access
Pets accepted; not in dining-room **Closed** Nov to mid-Dec
Languages English, French, Hungarian; some Italian
Proprietors Langs family

Steiermark

Castle hotel, Kapfenstein

Schlosswirt Kapfenstein

A steep road leads to this small castle that dates from the 11thC. Its hilltop position provided early warning of invading Turks and insurgent Hungarians centuries ago; nowadays, the view across rolling hills into Hungary and Slovenia is peaceful, with vineyards rather than armies marching in regular rows. The only guard to the former fortress is an amiable St. Bernard dog. The style is 'pleasant and comfortable rather than designer-deluxe'; nevertheless, guests give a high rating for the personal atmosphere. Martin and Elisabeth Winkler-Hermaden have run the hotel for over 20 years, establishing a reputation for hospitality that is matched by the quality of their wines.

On the 13.5 hectares (33 acres) of vineyards in south-west Styria, they grow ten types of grapes, including traditional Austrian varieties such as Traminer, Grauburgunder and Sauvignon Blanc. From the main variety, Blauen Zweigelt, comes their popular Olivin. This is left in barrels, made from local oak, stored in the 17thC *Löwenkeller*. Food is 'light, creative and Styrian', featuring game in the autumn, lamb in the spring, plus garden-grown herbs and vegetables.

Nearby Schloss Riegersburg, Schloss Kornberg.

8353 Kapfenstein
Tel (03157) 2202
Fax (03157) 22024
Location on peak of Kapfensteinerkogel; ample car parking
Meals breakfast, lunch, dinner, snacks
Prices DB&B from SSS
Rooms 8 double; all have bath or shower, central heating, phone, TV
Facilities 2 dining-rooms, sitting-room, TV room; 3 terraces
Credit Cards not accepted
Children very welcome
Disabled not suitable
Pets accepted
Closed Christmas, Feb
Languages English
Proprietors Winkler-Hermaden family

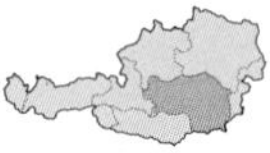

Steiermark

Vineyard hotel, Kitzeck

Weinhof Kappel

The recent conversion here of five bedrooms to *Biozimmern* reflects the influence of the Green movement in Styria. It comes as no surprise to us, since the dignified demeanour of Herr Kappel bespeaks a man who is serious about his business and serious about his wine. We were mightily impressed by this stylish modern hotel at the top of a steep, winding road.

Kitzeck, near the Slovenian border boasts that it is the highest wine-growing region in Europe (560 m) and it was the vineyard that brought Gunther Kappel here in the first place, some 25 years ago. The ancient wine-cellar, complete with splendidly carved and gilded casks, houses his pride and joy, especially the Welschriesling, the Muscatel and Morillon (or Chardonnay). The food is enterprising; a speciality is stuffed chicken breast in a Riesling sauce. Blue and white sunshades dot the leafy terrace outside; honey-coloured wood and pink tablecloths lend a comfortable yet formal air to the dining-room which has enviable vistas over the vineyards. Just as much care has been taken over the bedrooms which are bigger than average, often with balconies, pale pine panelling and pots of flowers.

Nearby vineyard.

8442 Kitzeck, Steinriegel 25
Tel (03456) 2347
Fax (03456) 234730
Location on hilltop among vines; ample car parking
Meals breakfast, lunch, dinner, snacks
Prices rooms SS-SSS with breakfast; reductions for children
Rooms 15 double, 1 single; all have bath or shower, central heating, phone, TV, radio
Facilities 2 dining-rooms, sitting-room, TV room; terrace
Credit Cards not accepted
Children welcome
Disabled not suitable
Pets not accepted
Closed Jan, Feb
Languages English
Proprietors Kappel family

Steiermark

❄ Rural hotel, Pruggern ❄

Farmreiterhof

Forget every tired cliché about alpine hotels and alpine vistas. This is the real thing. Deep in the countryside, the only morning sound we heard was the tinkling of cowbells in the pasture below the house. From our balcony, we watched deer scuttling from the garden into the pine forest.

No wonder we felt envious of the regulars who come here year after year to ski in winter and hike or climb the mountains in summer. The house dates from 1872 and has been in the family for five generations. The Gerharters are natural innkeepers, making little separation between their life and that of the guests. Heinrich teaches in the Federal Forestry and Agricultural School and also edits a local newspaper in Enns. Elisabeth runs the hotel with the help of the granny and the next generation is being primed to take over. The cooking is home-style and filling, with dishes such as *Kasnockerln* (cheese noodles) and *Ennstaler Krapfen* (doughnuts filled with brown crumbly cheese) which are best partnered by *Schnaps*. Peaks such as Grimming, Kammspitze and Dachstein provide names for the bedrooms which, like the rest of the hotel, have rustic, homely comforts.

Nearby winter sports; hiking, riding.

8965 Pruggern 65
Tel (03685) 22692
Fax (03685) 2333377
Location high above village; own car parking
Meals breakfast, snacks
Prices rooms S-SS with breakfast; reductions for children
Rooms 5 double; all have bath or shower, central heating, TV
Facilities dining-room, TV and sitting-room; terrace, outdoor heated swimming-pool; sauna
Credit Cards not accepted
Children very welcome
Disabled not suitable
Pets not accepted
Closed Christmas
Languages English, some French
Proprietors Gerharter family

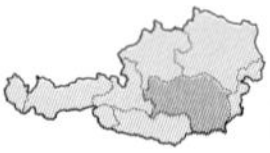

Steiermark

❄ Chalet hotel, Ramsau ❄

Peter Rosegger

A display of mountain-climbing equipment by the front door gives a clue to the favourite summer-time activity at this chalet-style inn, set on a plateau beneath the Dachstein ridge. Fritz Walcher is a well-known mountain guide and runs courses in climbing, starting with children as young as four years old and continuing to advanced level. In winter, he leads cross-country ski and snow-shoe safaris to secret valleys and huts.

As for the name, "we did not want another 'Dachsteinblick' or 'Alpenrose', so chose the famous Styrian romantic poet." Pictures relating to his life hang on the walls, while villages with a Rosegger connection provide names of bedrooms. All have a little entrance hall and large cupboards, while the family rooms at ground level have doors leading into the garden, so children (and pets) can go straight outside. The food is renowned; expect home-smoked trout, yoghurt and goat cheeses from local farms, and teas made from mountain herbs. Organic produce, vegetarian dishes and even flour-free recipes are all served up in the cosy dining-rooms where guests congregate for dinner.

Nearby Dachstein Tauern mountains; winter sports; hiking, climbing.

8972 Ramsau am Dachstein 233
Tel (03687) 81223
Fax (03687) 812238
Location on high plateau; approach via Kulm, follow signs to Vorberg; ample car-parking
Meals breakfast, lunch, dinner, snacks
Prices DB&B from SS-SSS
Rooms 6 double, 2 single, 5 family; all have central heating; some phone
Facilities dining-room, sitting-room, TV room, table-tennis room; terrace, garden; sauna
Credit Cards not accepted
Children very welcome
Disabled easy access **Pets** accepted **Closed** end Oct to mid-Dec; after Easter to end May **Languages** English, some French
Proprietors Fritz and Barbara Walcher

Steiermark

❄ **Restaurant with rooms, Riegersburg** ❄

Gasthof Fink

Riegersburg Castle has to be one of the world's most imposing fortresses, sitting on a granite ridge, scowling over the Styrian countryside. What a grim contrast it makes with the genuine jollity of the Fink family inn at the foot of the crag. The solid, white rectangular hotel with its green shutters and decorated walls also has panoramic views, especially from the restaurant. Here, Gottfried Fink and his sons serve the sort of Styrian specialities not found elsewhere in Austria. Favourites include the local roast beef with polenta.

Don't, however, expect fancy comforts. The Finks are very down-to-earth. Terracotta tiled floors in the entrance lead to the open-plan café, bar and sitting area. The *Stüberl,* a smaller dining-room with bench seats, cherry-wood veneer furniture and panelled ceiling is unashamedly rural. Some of the bedrooms are still rather dark; those remodelled back in 1989 are much lighter, with white walls and stripped-pine furniture. Outside, walnut and chestnut trees shade the terrace where parents relax, sipping the Styrian wines, while children enjoy home-made ice cream, and all tuck into the barbecue, accompanied by music.

Nearby castle with Witches' museum, birds of prey observatory.

8333 Riegersburg 29
Tel (03153) 8216
Fax (03153) 7357
Location on hilltop, below castle; own car parking
Meals breakfast, lunch, dinner, snacks
Prices rooms S-SS with breakfast; reductions for children
Rooms 26 double, 6 single; all have bath or shower, central heating, TV, radio, hairdrier; some phone
Facilities 5 dining-rooms, sitting-room, bar, billiard room; terrace
Credit Cards DC, MC, V
Children very welcome
Disabled not suitable
Pets accepted
Closed Feb; restaurant only, Tues
Languages English
Proprietors Fink family

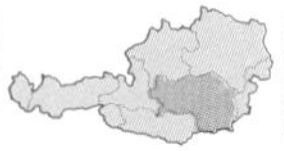

Steiermark

Castle hotel, Sebersdorf

Schlosshotel Obermayerhofen

'The honeymoon suite would not be beneath the dignity of Elizabeth Taylor' was our inspector's verdict. It was meant as a compliment, for he reckoned this hilltop hotel was 'the last word in luxury' and ideal for affluent romantics.

Bedrooms are named for the noble Austrian families and all are on a grand scale. Plain colours such as cream, butter-yellow and apricot provide the background for antiques and Persian carpets. Some have four-poster beds, in others swathes of fabric are draped from a coronet above the headboard. Even the bathrooms are generous in size, with potted plants, huge towels, and the latest in fittings, including some whirlpool baths.

A hotel only since 1986, the estate has been in the family of Count Kottulinsky since 1777. Like so many castles in Austria, its plain exterior contrasts with the Renaissance arcades and staircases of the inner courtyard. Indoors, chandeliers glitter, parquet floors shine with polish, and huge windows let in plenty of light. In the ceremonial hall, an 18thC fresco depicts a fanciful jungle scene, complete with palm trees and growling leopard. The private chapel may be used for weddings.

Nearby castles; wildlife park; Stift Vorau.

8272 Sebersdorf
Tel (03333) 25030
Fax (03333) 250350
Location on low hill, near Vienna-Graz motorway; own car parking
Meals breakfast, lunch, dinner
Prices rooms SSS-SSSS with breakfast; reductions for children **Rooms** 20 double; all have bath or shower, central heating, phone, TV, radio, minibar, hairdrier
Facilities 2 dining-rooms, sitting-room, bar, billiard room; terrace, park; beauty salon, sauna
Credit Cards AE, DC, MC, V
Children accepted but not ideal
Disabled not suitable
Pets not accepted
Closed early Jan to end Feb
Languages English, French, Italian
Proprietor Graf Kottulinsky

Steiermark

❄ **Rural hotel, Turnau** ❄

Frühstückspension Kirchleiten

'Like being mothered and pampered by a favourite aunt in the country' was our inspector's reaction to the welcome extended by Irmgard Knapp in her 'enchanting village house, with verandahs covered in different varieties of geraniums.' Her husband, Bernhardt, is one of a long line of master carpenters, which explains the lovingly-carved staircase and the distinctive light-and-dark pine panelling in the dining-room. The house dates back to 1750 when it was built as a *Bauernhof* (farmhouse) with the usual 2 cows, some pigs and chickens. Since 1954, the Knapp family have expanded and improved it, all with their own hands. Even the two life-sized straw men on the stairway were made by Frau Knapp for a local carnival 20 years ago.

Our inspector was particularly taken with the rooms in the old house, which have wood-panelling and small square windows; many also have balconies. At the very top are small, cosy rooms 'like a dolls' house.' The new suites, on the other hand, have white-washed walls and furniture of light-coloured pine with peasant floral decoration. Views are across the valley or over the garden with fruit trees and the village church behind.

Nearby riding school; winter sports; hang-gliding.

8625 Turnau 34
Tel (03863) 2234
Fax (03863) 2001
Location in heart of entrancing village in valley; own car parking
Meals breakfast, lunch, dinner, snacks
Prices rooms S-SS with breakfast; reductions for children
Rooms 10 double, 5 single; all have bath or shower, central heating, phone, TV, radio, minibar, kitchenette; some hairdrier
Facilities dining-room, sitting-room, bar; terrace
Credit Cards not accepted
Children very welcome
Disabled not suitable
Pets accepted
Closed Nov to mid-Dec
Languages English, French
Proprietors Knapp family

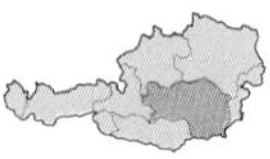

Steiermark

Restaurant with rooms, Weiz

Modernshof

The food is the main draw here. 'Refined Styrian' could mean a summer dinner of asparagus roulade and shrimp with noodles followed by a strawberry and wine sorbet. 'Excellent' was our verdict on a carefully-prepared meal, partnered by a local Traminer and eaten to the strains of Mozart's *Don Giovanni* enjoying his last meal. We were glad that it was not ours, since breakfast was another meal to be thoroughly enjoyed.

The only drawback is the curved staircase that descends into the dining-room; with people going up and down, any chance of an intimate dinner is lost.

The hotel was built in 1977 on the site of an old farmhouse. Tucked away in the hills and surrounded by orchards, it is an island of green. An attractive seating area behind the arched windows along the front is a pleasant place for coffee or before-dinner drinks. At the back, a yellow awning shades the terrace which looks out on the large swimming-pool.

We gave our bedroom a 'comfortable' rating for the modern furniture and prints by naive artists on the walls; we were less enthusiastic about the garish orange tiles in the bathroom.

Nearby riding; Raabklamm nature reserve; gliding.

8160 Weiz, Büchl 32
Tel (03172) 3747
Fax (03172) 37472
Location landscaped hotel in Styrian hills; ample car parking
Meals breakfast, lunch, dinner, snacks
Prices rooms SS-SSS with breakfast
Rooms 8 double; all have bath or shower, central heating, phone, TV, radio, hairdrier
Facilities 2 dining-rooms, sitting-room, bar; terrace, garden; sauna, outdoor swimming-pool
Credit Cards AE, DC, MC, V
Children accepted but not suitable
Disabled not suitable
Pets accepted
Closed 10 Jan to end March
Languages English, French, Italian, Spanish
Proprietors Mayer family

Steiermark

❄ Village inn, Aich ❄

Gasthof Bärenwirt

A picture of the God of Wine greets guests just inside the main entrance of this 16thC tavern. The Pilz family are proud of their food. Rooms are plain but comfortable. Skiing on Hauser Kaibling is 5 minutes away by car. Golf nearby.

■ 8966 Aich-Assach **Tel** (03686) 4303 **Fax** (03686) 430345
Meals breakfast, lunch, dinner, snacks **Prices** rooms S-SS with breakfast
Rooms 26, all with bath or shower, central heating, phone
Credit Cards not accepted **Closed** Oct, Mar **Languages** English

Village inn, Aigen im Ennstal

Gasthof Putterersee

This 250-year old village inn had a total facelift in 1995. Family-oriented, this is a safe, friendly spot for children with its large garden. Windsurfers and boats are available on the small lake. Popular also as a base for fishermen, cyclists and walkers.

■ 8943 Aigen im Ennstal 13 **Tel** (03682) 22520 **Fax** (03682) 2252033
Meals breakfast, lunch, dinner, snacks **Prices** rooms S-SS with breakfast
Rooms 18, all with bath or shower, central heating, phone, TV, radio
Credit Cards not accepted **Closed** Nov **Languages** English, Italian

❄ Town hotel, Bad Aussee ❄

Villa Kristina

Everything about this 100-year old house is turn-of-the-century, from the furnishings to the dignified politeness of silver-haired owner, Friedl Raudaschl. Although regulars have been coming back for 30 years, newcomers are welcomed. Light cooking.

■ 8990 Bad Aussee **Tel and Fax** (03622) 52017 **Meals** breakfast, dinner, snacks **Prices** rooms S-SSS with breakfast **Rooms** 12, all with bath or shower, central heating, phone, TV **Credit Cards** AE, DC, MC, V
Closed early Nov to mid-Dec **Languages** English, French, Italian, Spanish

❄ Family hotel, Bad Mitterndorf ❄

Hotel Kogler

The Koglers have been specializing in children's holidays in the Salzkammergut for 40 years. They have recently added a new indoor swimming-pool, sauna, solarium, as well as 2 tennis-courts. Nannies entertain children with walks, cycle rides.

■ 8983 Bad Mitterndorf **Tel** (03623) 23250 **Fax** (03623) 3107
Meals breakfast, lunch, dinner, snacks **Prices** DB&B SS **Rooms** 31, all with bath or shower, central heating, phone, TV **Credit Cards** not accepted **Closed** Nov to mid-Dec; 2 weeks after Easter **Languages** English

Steiermark

❄ Farmhouse hotel, Gröbming ❄

Landgasthof Reisslerhof

Surrounded by fields, with a working farm and riding school next door, this is ideal for familes. Rooms are modern, spacious. Heated swimming-pool, health and fitness facilities, plus organic dishes. Tennis nearby and ski-slopes only a 10-minute drive.

■ 8962 Gröbming-Mitterberg **Tel** (03685) 22364 **Fax** (03685) 2236410 **Meals** breakfast, lunch, dinner, snacks **Prices** rooms S-SS with breakfast **Rooms** 25, all with shower, central heating, phone **Credit Cards** not accepted **Closed** Nov **Languages** English, French, some Italian

Lakeside guest-house, Grundlsee

Gasthof Ladner

On the Grundlsee lake, near the cable-car up to the Appelhaus, this 200-year old inn is an inexpensive base for walkers who explore the Totes Gebirge mountains. Christine Grill is known for her wholesome cooking and home-made cakes.

■ 8993 Grundlsee, Gössl 1 **Tel** (03622) 8211 **Fax** (03622) 82114 **Meals** breakfast, lunch, dinner, snacks **Prices** rooms S-SS with breakfast **Rooms** 6, all with shower; TV on request **Credit Cards** AE **Closed** mid-Nov to early Dec; March; restaurant only, Wed **Languages** English, French, Italian, Dutch

❄ Country hotel, Kitzeck ❄

Pension Steirerland

Although the building is a standard, modern chalet, it boasts a striking hill-top position, with views to the Slovenian Alps and a huge, covered terrace. Meals are delicious, Styrian-style, with unusual wine soups. Ruth Stelzer is a charming hostess.

■ 8442 Kitzeck, Höch am Demmerkogel **Tel** (03456) 2328 **Fax** (03456) 232828 **Meals** breakfast, lunch, dinner, snacks **Prices** rooms S-SS with breakfast **Rooms** 10, all with bath or shower, central heating, phone, TV, radio **Credit Cards** not accepted **Closed** Jan, Feb **Languages** English, French

❄ Country guest-house, Krakauebene ❄

Haus Schaller

Children enjoy playing with the chickens and goats; cross-country skiers stop at local farmhouses for a Schnaps; families go for sleigh-rides. The Schnedlitz's simple hotel is a place to relax, high in the Tauern range. Own tennis court.

■ 8854 Krakauebene 55, Klausen **Tel and Fax** (03535) 334 **Meals** breakfast, lunch, dinner, snacks **Prices** rooms S with breakfast **Rooms** 13, all with bath or shower, central heating **Credit Cards** not accepted **Closed** Nov to mid-Dec; May **Languages** English

Steiermark

❊ Farmhouse inn, Krieglach ❊

Annerlbauerhof

Stuffed animals and open fires greet guests. Upstairs, old-fashioned Alpine-style bedrooms and split-level apartments are rather dark. Honest country cooking. Floodlit ski trails on the doorstep. Ideal for low-cost, unpretentious outdoor holidays.

■ 8670 Krieglach, Malleisten 15 **Tel** (03855) 2228 **Fax** (03855) 222820 **Meals** breakfast, lunch, dinner, snacks **Prices** rooms S-SS with breakfast **Rooms** 13, all with bath or shower; TV on request **Credit Cards** not accepted **Closed** mid-Oct to mid-Nov; Easter **Languages** German only

❊ Bed-and-breakfast hotel, Mariazell ❊

Mariazellerhof

Mariazell is Austria's main pilgrimage destination. The Pirker family's hotel is only 200 m west of the 14thC basilica. Built in 1969, it is modern, but also cheerful and comfortable. Ski-school and Bürgeralpe slopes within walking distance.

■ 8630 Mariazell **Tel** (03882) 2179 **Fax** (03882) 217951 **Meals** breakfast **Prices** rooms S-SS with breakfast **Rooms** 10, all with bath or shower, central heating, phone, TV **Credit Cards** DC, MC **Closed** never **Languages** English

❊ Converted Alpine hut, Mühlen ❊

Tonnerhütte und Gästehaus

Our intrepid inspector drove up 'a vertical, unmetalled road to a mountain hut at the end of the world'. Fabulous views from Jakobsberg across the valley. Rustic rooms. Some skiing, nearby lift, no crowds. Perfect for getting back to nature. Inexpensive.

■ 8822 Mühlen, Jakobsberg 2 **Tel** (03584) 3250 **Meals** breakfast, lunch, dinner, snacks **Prices** rooms S-SS with breakfast **Rooms** 5, with shower; 5, with wash-basins **Credit Cards** not accepted **Closed** Nov; 3 weeks after Easter **Languages** English, Italian

❊ Family-hotel, Murau ❊

Murauer Gasthof-Hotel Lercher

In an old town in Western Styria, this traditional inn manages to be all things to all guests. There is a gourmet candle-light dinner on the first Saturday of the month, a children's Stammtisch, wine-tasting, musical evenings. Skiing nearby.

■ 8850 Murau, Schwarzenbergstr 10 **Tel** (03532) 2431 **Fax** (03532) 3694 **Meals** breakfast, lunch, dinner, snacks **Prices** rooms SS-SSS with breakfast **Rooms** 26, all with bath or shower, central heating, phone, TV **Credit Cards** AE, DC, MC, V **Closed** never **Languages** English, French, Italian

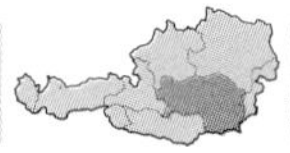

Steiermark

❄ Country inn, Mürzsteg ❄

Gasthof-Pension Schönauer

Although the Treaty of Macedonia was signed here by the Russian tsar and the Austro-Hungarian emperor, this inn is now known for owner Meta Schönauer's cooking. Own tennis court; cross-country ski trails from the door; ski school nearby.

■ 8693 Mürzsteg **Tel** (03859) 2214 **Meals** breakfast, lunch, dinner, snacks **Prices** rooms S with breakfast **Rooms** 9, all with bath or shower, central heating **Credit Cards** not accepted **Closed** mid-Oct to mid-Nov **Languages** German only

❄ Mountain hotel, near Obdach ❄

Judenburger Hütte

Approaching this remote mountain retreat, deer leap across the steep road through the woods. The tennis court is the highest in Styria (1420 m). Cross-country skiing from the door. Large indoor swimming-pool with sauna/solarium. Barbecue evenings.

■ 8742 St Wolfgang am Zirbitz, Obdach **Tel and Fax** (03578) 8202 **Meals** breakfast, lunch, dinner, snacks **Prices** rooms S-SS with breakfast **Rooms** 16, all with bath or shower, central heating **Credit Cards** not accepted **Closed** 3 weeks Nov; 3 weeks April **Languages** English, French, Italian

Village inn, Obdach

Groggerhof

On the main street of Obdach, this 360-year old inn has a growing reputation for its food thanks to Eva Ederer-Grogger. Visitors and locals enjoy her authentic Styrian cooking, with as many as a dozen wines available by the glass.

■ 8742 Obdach, Hauptplatz **Tel** (03578) 2201 **Fax** (03578) 2660 **Meals** breakfast, lunch, dinner, snacks **Prices** rooms S-SS with breakfast **Rooms** 15, all with bath or shower, central heating, phone, TV **Credit Cards** not accepted **Closed** never; restaurant only, Mon **Languages** English, French, Italian

Bakery with rooms, Puch bei Weiz

Landgasthof Eitljörg

The mouth-watering scent of fresh baking greets guests to this 100-year old hotel in the heart of Styria's apple-orchards. Bedrooms in the older building are nicely old-fashioned. Special apple diets, apple *Schnaps*, apple *Sekt.*

■ 8182 Puch bei Weiz **Tel** (03177) 2204 **Fax** (03177) 3225 **Meals** breakfast, lunch, dinner, snacks **Prices** rooms S-SS with breakfast **Rooms** 14, all with bath or shower, central heating; TV on request **Credit Cards** MC **Closed** Nov or Jan **Languages** English

Steiermark

Old inn, St Gallen

Gasthof Hensle

This solid green-painted inn has faced the square with its statue of John of Nepomuk for centuries. Although the *Stüberl* which doubles as the breakfast-room has beams dated 1509, the bedrooms are modern and functional. A useful overnight stop.

■ 8933 St Gallen 43 **Tel** (03632) 7171 **Fax** (03632) 717123 **Meals** breakfast, lunch, dinner, snacks **Prices** rooms S-SS with breakfast **Rooms** 16, all with bath or shower, central heating, phone, TV, radio **Credit Cards** AE, DC, MC **Closed** first week Sept; restaurant only, Wed **Languages** English

❄ Modern hotel, Stadl an der Mur ❄

Murtalerhof

Bright, new hotel; rather lacking in character. However, Johann Lassacher prepares authentic Styrian dishes, much appreciated by rafting enthusiasts who hurtle down the Mur river. Cavernous dining-room; plain bedrooms. Skiing at Kreischberg, 5 km.

■ 8862 Stadl an der Mur, Steindorf 11 **Tel** (03534) 2237 **Fax** (03534) 223744 **Meals** breakfast, lunch, dinner, snacks **Prices** rooms S-SS with breakfast **Rooms** 23, all with bath or shower, central heating, phone, TV, hairdrier **Credit Cards** not accepted **Closed** never **Languages** English, French, Italian

❄ Medieval inn, near Stein/Enns ❄

Gasthof 'Zum Gamsjäger'

This 13thC inn has been carefully modernized by the Trischer family who kept some Gothic features, such as the ceilings. A truly well-priced base for exploring the breathtaking Sölk pass, the Sölktaler park. Pale pinks, blues, pine wood in bedrooms.

■ 8961 Stein/Enns, St Nikolai 127 **Tel** (03689) 210 **Meals** breakfast, lunch, dinner, snacks **Prices** rooms S with breakfast **Rooms** 17, all with bath or shower, central heating, radio; TV by request **Credit Cards** not accepted **Closed** Nov to 20 Dec **Languages** German only

Index of hotel names

In this index, hotels are arranged in order of the most distinctive part of their name; in many cases, other parts of the name are also given after the main part, but very common prefixes such as 'Hotel', 'Gasthof' and 'Das' are omitted. Where a hotel's name begins with Schloss or Schlosshotel, it will normally be indexed under the word that follows.

Index of hotel names

Index of hotel names

Near Salzburg For visitors who prefer to stay near the city, rather than in it, we list the towns where we have recommended hotels within about 80 km/1 hour's drive of Salzburg. Most are in Salzburgerland, listed between pages 62 and 85:

Abtenau, Altenmarkt, Dorfgastein, Filzmoos, Fuschl am See, Goldegg, Hallein, Leogang, Mattsee, Oberalm, St Gilgen, Strasswalchen, Wagrain and Werfen. There are three towns in Oberösterreich, listed between pages 86 and 104. In Styria, Altaussee (pages 164/165) is 80 km from Salzburg.

Near Vienna For visitors who prefer to stay near the capital, rather than in it, we list the towns where we have recommended hotels within about 80 km/1 hour's drive of Vienna. Some are in Niederösterreich, listed between pages 105 and 124:

Baden, Dürnstein, Klein-Wien, Klosterneuberg, Krems, Laaben, Mautern, Mayerling, Payerbach, Puchberg am Schneeberg, Tullnerbach and Weissenkirchen.

The rest are in Burgenland, listed between paged 136 and 142:

Eisenstadt, Gols, Mörbisch, Neusiedl and Purbach.

Index of hotel locations

In this index, hotels are arranged by the name of city, town or village they are in or near. Where a hotel is located in a very small place, it may be indexed under a nearby place which is more easily found on maps. Hotels in well-known resort areas such as Attersee or Faakersee are listed under the lake in general, then the specific village.

Index of hotel locations

Index of hotel locations

Reporting to the guides

Please write and tell us about your experiences of small hotels, guest-houses and inns, whether good or bad, whether listed in this edition or not. As well as hotels in Austria, we are interested in charming small hotels in: Britain, Ireland, Italy, France, Spain, Portugal, Germany, Switzerland and other European countries, as well as the east and west coasts of the United States.

The address to write to us is:

The Editors,
Austria,
Charming Small Hotel Guides,
Duncan Petersen Publishing Ltd,
31 Ceylon Road,
London, W14 OPY
England.

Checklist
Please use a separate sheet of paper for each report; include your name, address and telephone number on each sheet.

Your reports are particularly welcome if they are typed and organized under the following headings:

Name of establishment
Town or village
Full address and post code
Telephone number
Time and duration of visit
The building and setting
Public rooms
Bedrooms and bathrooms
Standards of maintenance, housekeeping
Standards of comfort and decoration
Atmosphere, welcome and service
Food
Value for money

We assume that in writing you have no objection to your views being published unpaid, either verbatim or in an edited version. Names of major outside contributors are acknowledged in the guide, at the editor's discretion.